The Royal Celtic Society
1820–2020

Priscilla Scott

CHA TRÉIG MI THU

First published in Great Britain in 2020 by
The Royal Celtic Society
Edinburgh
www.royalcelticsociety.scot

ISBN: 978 1 5272 5133 5

British Library Cataloguing-in-Publication Data
A catalogue record for this book is available on request from the British Library

Designed and typeset by Edderston Book Design, Peebles
Printed and bound in Wales by Gwasg Gomer, Llandysul, Ceredigion

This book, relating the history of the Royal Celtic Society over the last 200 years, is the story of the survival of Scotland's cultural heritage. From the society's initial objective to remind Highland Scots of their traditional dress following the repeal of the Act of Proscription, through its ground-breaking activity in supporting education in the Highlands, to its wider role today in promoting and defending Scotland's history, traditions, languages and arts, the society has been for two centuries at the heart of activity to preserve that which makes Scotland what she is.

As Dr. Scott relates, it is the story of a society that was, in many respects, ahead of its time. It was one of the first educational prize-givers to allow girls to compete on equal terms. The society was among the first to offer educational prizes on a cross-denominational basis, in an era when most such recognition was restricted to schools of the established Church of Scotland. It was equally inclusive of those from beyond our shores: the secretary wrote in 1823 that membership was open to all 'whose heart warms to the tartan, of whatever country, kindred or religion'. Later, the Royal Celtic Society would become a great champion of Gaelic, during the Clearance period and following the 1872 Education Act, when the language arguably faced its greatest trial.

It is the story of a society that has had to adapt to a changing world. It has stood the test of time, when others have not, because it has never been afraid to re-invent itself in response to changing circumstances. Throughout its history, the Royal Celtic Society has succeeded in evolving its activities in response to the needs of the time. Through its commitment today to the future of piping, clarsach, poetry, literature and language, it continues to play its part in ensuring the long-term future of the rich heritage we are all proud to share. As I take up office as the Royal Celtic Society's Patron in its 200th birthday year, I look forward to supporting its work in ensuring Scotland's distinctive cultural tradition endures for the 200 years to come.

Anne

Detail from Kirkwood's *Plan & Elevation of the New Town of Edinburgh, 1819*: the approximate site of Oman's Tavern, where the first meeting of the Celtic Society took place on 7 January 1820, is marked ✻ and New Register House (opened 1861), where the society's lectures now take place, is marked with a square

Introduction

The Celtic Society (it received its 'Royal' designation from Queen Victoria in 1873) was formed in 1820 in the cultural and intellectual metropolis that was post-Enlightenment Edinburgh. Its inaugural objective was to restore and promote the 'general use of the Ancient Highland Dress of the Highlanders of Scotland', but this central focus was extended over the years to embrace further objectives 'connected with the preservation of the characteristics of the Highlanders'. Other societies of the period had similar interests and a similarly elite membership profile, two of the most prestigious being the Highland societies of London (1778) and Scotland (1784). Both attracted influential members from the aristocracy and landed gentry, many of whom were serving or former officers in the British Army. The Highland Society of Scotland was also based in Edinburgh, and there was a degree of overlap in membership between it and the Celtic Society, but the latter was never as big, and its aims were more modest.

The post-Culloden Disclothing Act, which outlawed the wearing of tartan as plaid or kilt, stripped Highlanders of a fabric and dress – *am breacan uallach* 'the proud plaid' – that were embedded in their history and increasingly symbolic of their identity and of the very spirit of resistance which the Act had been designed to quell. The penalties for infringement were severe, and the Act achieved its objective. The one arena where the wearing of Highland dress was allowed to continue was the army, where the government recognised that the perceived 'martial spirit' of the tartan-clad Highlander could be usefully redeployed. Thus it proved. With the adoption of tartan as the distinctive uniform of the Highland regiments from the eighteenth century onwards, the wearing of Highland dress became increasingly associated with their reputation for bravery and fierce loyalty in battle. By the time the tartan restriction was lifted in 1782, the case for its repeal having been brought before parliament by the Marquis of Graham, the Jacobite cause and those who fought for it had taken on a much softer focus in the eyes of the establishment. This romantic reappraisal offered an opening for the dress of the Highlander, with all its previous negative associations of barbarity and opposition, to be transformed into a much more acceptable cultural commodity, one that could be safely embraced as a distinctive emblem of Scottishness within the wider circle of the Union. Not surprisingly, however, given the severity of Cumberland's post-Culloden reprisals, the wearing of tartan and kilt had more or less ceased amongst the general populace of the Highlands; those that had known it as an everyday garment were by 1820 very few, and while the repeal of the Act was greeted with great joy, as celebrated in many Gaelic songs, a generation had grown up in the Highlands since 1746 who had little experience of making or wearing tartan either as plaid or kilt.

While the Highland societies of London and Scotland were concerned with the tartan issue, both had broader aims as well. In contrast, the Celtic Society had, at the beginning at least, the exclusive objective of encouraging the general use of 'the Ancient Highland Dress' in the Highlands. This was explained in detail at the first General Meeting in 1820:

> It is true that the Highland Society established [in Edinburgh] has done much for the improvement of the Highlands, for the ameliorating of the condition of its inhabitants and for the preservation of some of its ancient manners and customs and it merits therefore and enjoys and long may it enjoy most extensive support – but its objects are so numerous, that in one department its success although certain from the ability of the gentlemen who superintend it, is assuredly slow. Now this Society seeks to avoid this common shipwreck of Utility – it limits itself strictly to one object, and therefore increases the probability of accomplishing it.

How exactly this 'one object' would be achieved was not made clear, and the society, as will be seen, soon realised that it needed to identify a more structured and directly beneficial philanthropic project into which the wearing of Highland dress could be incorporated.

The narrative of this book draws closely on the papers of the Royal Celtic Society that were gifted to the National Library of Scotland in 2018 (Acc. 13898). This valuable archive of minute books, accounts, letters and associated papers provides a detailed record of the society, its membership and its activities from 1820 to 1968. It also offers a specific window on the changing social and cultural environment of Edinburgh through the nineteenth century and into the modern period, and on influential individuals and networks within the metropolis – their perspectives on the Highlands, and the ways in which these altered through time and circumstance. The story of the society is one of continuity and change in its objectives and profile, and of ebb and flow in membership and momentum. It has, however, remained rooted in the city of its birth across the 200 years it has now been in existence, and it is against the backdrop of the cultural, intellectual and physical landscape of the Scottish capital that its history unfolds.

To Capt. William MacKenzie, founder of the Celtic Society

'S mi 'm shuidh' an seo 'm ònar
    Ann an seòmar leam fhéin
A' snìomh éide don òigear
    'S deise còmhnairde ceum,
Do Chaiptean MacCoinnich,
    Fear foghainteach treun,
'S chan eil mulad no bròn orm
    Gun duine 'm chòir bheir dhomh sgeul.

I'm sitting here alone
    In a room by myself
Spinning clothes for the handsome
    Smooth-stepping hero,
For Captain MacKenzie,
    An able, brave man,
And I don't mind having no one
    Here to give me their news.

Nam b' urrainn mi 'n òran,
    Dheilbhinn còmhradh le rùin
Mun fhear 's maisich 'm measg còisre
    'Ga bheil foghlam is iùl —
'S ann a ghabh mi ort eòlas
    Aig a' chòmhdhail an tùs
'S bu lìonmhor baintighearn' 's math stoidhle
    A bha faighneachd co thù.

If I were able in song,
    I'd talk eagerly of him
Who's the best-looking member
    Of the wise learned society —
I got to know you
    First at the gathering
Where lots of elegant ladies
    Asked who you were.

'S math thig breacan an fhéilidh
    Mu do shléistean gu dlùth,
Osain gheàrr agus gartain
    Nach d'thig faisg air a' ghlùin,
Agus còta dhen tartan
    Air a bhasadh mu d' chùl
'S ite dhosrach an fhìreoin
    'S i gu dìreach á d' chrùn.

The kilt and the plaid
    Fit well round your thighs,
The short hose with garters
    Not too close to the knee,
With a waistcoat of tartan
    Passed round your back
And a plumed eagle's feather
    Rising up from your head.

Air a' choinnimh 'n Dùn Éideann
  Measg nan ceud fhuair thu cliù
Aig grinnead do phearsa
  'S do dhreas air do chùl;
Cha robh leithid MhicCoinnich
  Sa cho-thional an tùs —
Thug Rìgh Deòrsa dha 'n t-urram
  Thar gach duine fon chrùn:

At the Edinburgh meeting
  You were famed amongst hundreds
For your personal elegance
  And the clothes on your back;
There was none like MacKenzie
  To the fore in the gathering —
King George gave him honour
  Over all 'neath the crown:

Thug e òrdugh dh'fhear-làimh
  Dealbh 'n àrmainn chur suas
Ann an deise a' Ghàidhil
  Mar a bhà e san uair;
Do chomisean chaidh àrdach'
  Gu bhith 'd cheannard air sluagh,
Do chur air thoiseach nan Gàidheal
  Chumail 'n àird an t-sròil uain'.

He ordered an artist
  To paint our man's picture
In the garb of the Gael
  As he was at the time,
And you were promoted
  To be an army commander
At the head of the Gael
  And bear the green satin flag.

The Gaelic song of which these verses form a part was composed by Anna Ghobha (Anna Gow, 1788–*c*.1850), a native of Rannoch. It appears in Duncan Mackintosh's *Co-Chruinneach dh' Orain Thaghte Ghaeleach* (Edinburgh, 1831), pp. 99–102. Anna Gow is known to have been a highly skilled weaver of fine tartans, whose services were much in demand by the gentry for the production of the specialist fabrics needed for military uniforms and Highland dress. Perhaps the first 'gathering' she refers to was one of the society's school competitions in Perthshire, attended by male and female gentry.

In the fourth verse here Gow comes to George IV's visit. Her statement that the king ordered an artist to paint MacKenzie's picture is corroborated by John Prebble, who describes him as follows (*The King's Jaunt*, p. 116): "Said to be one of the most handsome men in the Highlands, he was a stately, aging man who did indeed look well in a belted plaid. So well, in fact, that when the King saw him at Holyrood he asked for the old man's portrait to be painted, and sent to him in England as an illustration of how a Highlander should look." The whereabouts of this picture is unknown, but it could be the watercolour shown at p. 15 below.

The 'promotion to army commander' described by Gow refers to MacKenzie's leadership of the military-style guard formed by members of the Celtic Society during the king's visit. It was indeed MacKenzie's task to carry the satin banner formally presented to him by Scott, but why should Gow call it green when it was principally white (or, as Prebble says, 'bright in many hues')? The probable reason is that she was influenced by Gaelic tradition to think of the Celtic Society as the Féinn, a mythical band of warriors led by Fionn mac Cumhail. They wandered free and had many adventures, but came to the aid of the worldly kingdom whenever it had need of them. Green, a difficult and unstable dye, is the otherworld colour, and the green flag may symbolise a sense of pan-Gaelic nationhood.

A Victorian Society: 1820–1882

CONSOLIDATION AND CONTROVERSY: THE FIRST TWO YEARS (1820-1822)

The founder of the Celtic Society, Captain William MacKenzie of Gruinard (1771–c.1848), is often overlooked in references to its origins in favour of the more flamboyant and public figures of Sir Walter Scott and Col. David Stewart of Garth. MacKenzie had served in the 72nd regiment of foot, but by 1820 he was retired on half pay and living in Edinburgh. His background in the British Army, and his historical family connections to the '45 through his MacKenzie grandfather, were important factors in nurturing his idea to establish 'a National Society in the Metropolis of Scotland for the purpose of encouraging a return of the ancient dress in the Highland Districts of the country'. Finding that there was support for his proposal, he invited a small group of sympathetic and influential gentlemen to a meeting in Oman's Tavern, 29 West Register St., Edinburgh, on 7 January 1820. Those present in addition to himself were the Hon. James Sinclair, Col. David Stewart of Garth, Robert Gordon, William Mackenzie of Strathgarve, Hugh Macdonald of Boisdale, Robert Roy, Hugh Fraser of Struie, Archibald Fraser of Abertarff, and an Edinburgh lawyer called Joseph Gordon. The first 'General Meeting' was planned for March that year, and as there was a need to ensure that a good number of gentlemen had signed up by that date, a flurry of meetings took place to nominate, ballot and admit members. At one such meeting on 26 January Garth stated that 'he was most happy in having the honor to announce to the Meeting, his being authorised to propose for admission into the Society a Candidate so distinguished as Walter Scott Esquire'. The celebrated writer was instantly admitted by acclamation, thus bypassing the normal membership procedure, and he remained an influential presence in the society throughout its earliest years.

The first membership lists show that this was an elite gentlemen's club. Its members were drawn from the highest level of the Highland aristocracy, the landowning gentry, the officer caste of the British army, and the professional classes of Edinburgh, the law being particularly well represented. These social networks

Charles Oman (a Caithness man) and his wife Grace were upwardly mobile Edinburgh hoteliers. They began with the premises in West Register St. where the first meeting of the Celtic Society took place, then leased Oman's London Hotel at 22 St Andrew St. In 1822, when they gave these up and took the lease of the Waterloo Hotel (with tavern and coffee-house) in Waterloo Place, the society moved its general meetings and dinners to that venue. About the same time the Omans purchased first no. 6 and then no. 4 in the prestigious Charlotte Square, where in 1825 they opened Oman's Hotel. It attracted a very elite clientele. Charles died in that same year, on which his wife gave up the Waterloo but continued to run Oman's in Charlotte Square. It is now Bute House, the official residence of the First Minister of Scotland.

The only known portrait of Oman is by the engraver John Kay (1742–1826). It requires some explanation, because he is the little fellow on the big fellow's back. What happened was this: a lawyer called Hamilton Bell, a big burly man, had bet his friend Edward Innes, a baker and confectioner, that even if he were carrying a person on his shoulders he could beat him walking the 12 miles (17 km) from Edinburgh to Musselburgh and back. The person so 'honoured'

was Oman, then a mere vintner's boy, though immaculately dressed. In Kay's drawing they are accompanied by John Rae, a dentist, carrying a bottle, and are passing a pair of fishwives carrying their wares to Edinburgh. As the drawing gave rise to widespread hilarity, Bell and Rae sued Kay for defamation, but the case was thrown out on the basis that the event had actually taken place.

The society's first president, the Marquis of Huntly, painted by George Sanders around 1827 when he became 5th Duke of Gordon

were closely interconnected, and through them the membership increased rapidly. The list of the first office-bearers neatly encapsulates the membership profile throughout the nineteenth century. The president, the Marquis of Huntly (1770–1836), was the first in a long line of prominent members of the aristocracy to fill that prime position, accepting the role on two further occasions in the 1830s, by which time he had inherited the title of Duke of Gordon. There were four vice-presidents: Col. David Stewart of Garth (1772–1829) was an officer in the 42nd Highlanders, later the Black Watch, and author of *Sketches of the Highlanders*, an influential book in promoting the iconic image of the Highland soldier (both his grandfathers had fought at Culloden, and he was inspired by this personal Jacobite history); Sir John MacGregor Murray (1745–1822) had had a military career in India, was chief of the Clan Gregor from 1775, and was a founding and influential member of the Highland Society of Scotland; John Norman MacLeod of Dunvegan (1788–1835) was 24th chief of his clan; and the fourth vice-president was Sir Walter Scott (1771–1832). William MacKenzie was the secretary, and Joseph Gordon, who had sold his small estate in Sutherland in 1812 to set up his law firm in Edinburgh,[1] was the treasurer, remaining in that role for over thirty years.

The first General Meeting took place on 3 March 1820, in Oman's London Hotel, where many of the public dinners in the city took place at that time. It was attended by seventy-three members, who had been strictly instructed to appear in Highland

11

Walter Scott is admitted 'by Acclamation', 26 January 1820

dress. In the absence of the president, Stewart of Garth took the chair. The business was to confirm the society's regulations and objectives, after which 'the gentlemen arrayed in full tartan adjourned to the dining room, and the meeting was prolonged to a late hour in the utmost hilarity and conviviality'. The Celtic Society was now officially inaugurated, and in reporting on this and on the amount of tartan sported by its members, the *Glasgow Herald* noted: "There has not since the '45, as we heard a venerable member exultingly and with much truth exclaim, been such a sight seen in the capital of our country." Among a long list of toasts throughout the inaugural dinner was one proposed by Scott to the health of the Duke of Montrose (being particularly honoured for his role, as Marquis of Graham, in bringing about the repeal of the 'Disclothing Act') in which he was perhaps being overly candid in seeking to reconcile his political and cultural loyalties:

> Within his own recollection, for no greater crime than appearing in that dress which had been worn by his Highland Ancestors for time immemorial, a Highlander would have been subjected to the punishment of a felon. This was certainly a degrading law, although he must presume it was at the time a necessary one.[2]

After the meeting a copy of the Rules and Regulations was sent out to actual and potential members; the accompanying letter offers an insight into the perspectives underpinning the main object of the organisation.

> It appears to the Gentlemen of the Society to be of much importance that the Highlanders should continue to wear this most ancient and characteristic Dress of their country. It is known to have a material effect in cherishing the martial spirit of the people, and the proverbial influence of the "*Tartan*" and of the associations combined with it, on the general character of the Highlanders, and on them when in the field, is universally acknowledged. That the Dress has of late years fallen much into disuse, is no less true than generally regretted; and there is too much cause for apprehension that unless encouraged now, it may at no distant period cease altogether to be the garb of the Highlander.

David Stewart of Garth (1772–1829), an eminent Gaelic-speaking landowner and antiquarian, had a distinguished military career. His two-volume *Sketches of the Character, Manners, and Present State of the Highlanders of Scotland* (1822) is a detailed account of the formation and military service of the Highland regiments, with information on other aspects of Highland life. It is still a valuable historical resource today. He was involved in compiling a register of tartans for the Highland Society of London, a collection that influenced subsequent ideas on specific clan tartans. Although he moved in the circles of his class, he had a great respect for the Highland people, and was remarkably outspoken against the Highland clearances. His time with the Celtic Society was influential but short, as he left Scotland to become Governor of St Lucia in 1826, and died there in 1829.

Minutes of a Meeting of Gentlemen connected with the Highlands of Scotland held at Oman's Tavern, Edinburgh, on the 7th of January 1820. —

Present,

The Honble James Sinclair 92nd Regt.
Colonel David Stuart of Garth,
Robert Gordon Esquire
William MacKenzie Esquire of Strathgarve,
William MacKenzie Esquire A.P. 72 Regt.
Hugh MacDonald Esquire of Boisdale,
Robert Roy Esquire,
Hugh Fraser Esquire, Struie,
Archibald Fraser Esquire of Abertarph
Joseph Gordon Esquire, Writer to the Signet.

Mr MacKenzie A.P.72 Regt. stated that it had occurred to him, and he had the pleasure of finding the Idea approved of by many respectable Gentlemen, connected with the Highlands of Scotland, in Edinburgh, that a National Society should be established in the Metropolis of Scotland for the purpose of encouraging a return to the ancient Dress in the Highland Districts of the Country—and the present meeting having

'A National Society should be established in the Metropolis of Scotland for the purpose of encouraging a return to the ancient Dress in the Highland Districts of the Country': the first meeting, 7 January 1820

It was agreed that, in order to build up its membership and accumulate revenue, the society would not undertake any philanthropic projects during its first two years. These two years, however, were not uneventful.

In May 1820, an 'Address to the Throne' offered the society's congratulations to the new king, George IV, and during his visit to Edinburgh in August 1822, its members

'Members whose dresses were ready should turn out in complete Highland Costume': sketch by David Wilkie of persons taking part in George IV's visit to Edinburgh, 1822

were given a prominent role. The event was stage-managed by Scott, ably assisted and advised by Garth, and the Celtic Society was given particular responsibility for guarding the Regalia of Scotland. In preparation, those taking part were instructed to attend drill every morning and evening in the parks between Queen St. and Heriot Row, with the instruction that 'members whose dresses were ready should turn out in complete Highland Costume', highlighting the fact that a number of those taking part did not possess Highland dress and had to order their 'costumes' for the occasion. Two white satin standards showing the blue St Andrew's cross in the star of the thistle and bearing the Gaelic words *Albainn mo ghraidh* ('O Scotia, my love') had been obtained, and these were formally presented to William MacKenzie and the Hon. James Sinclair by Scott and Garth respectively. Flags were also purchased for the additional pipers engaged to do duty along with the society's own piper, William MacKay.

Nowhere was the new-found respectability of the tartan-clad Highlander more evident than in the pageantry of this occasion, and the impressive appearance of the Celtic Society can be pictured from this newspaper report:

'Ask for the Celtic Guard'

Alexander Stuart (1786–1869) was a farmer's son from Rafford in Morayshire who trained as a 'writer' (solicitor) in Forres. In 1802, aged 16, he came to Edinburgh to join the legal firm run by another Morayshire man, Robert Gordon WS. He subsequently became a partner of Joseph Gordon of Carroll WS, first treasurer of the Celtic Society (their firm, Gordon & Stuart, was run from Bellevue Crescent). Alexander became secretary of the society, and the successor firm, Stuart & Stuart, has continued to provide it with secretaries or treasurers until 2020. When George IV visited Edinburgh in 1822, from 15 to 29 August, Alexander was one of the Celtic Society members who, suitably clothed as Highlanders, formed the king's guard at Holyrood Palace. The two letters opposite were written home to his wife Mary on that occasion. 'Hector' and 'Peggy' are presumably servants. 'Joseph' is their son Joseph Gordon Stuart (1815–66), then aged seven. Who 'Maria' and 'Mary Thomson' are is not known.

Alexander Stuart

Send me two or three
sheets of paper

My dear Mary
Be so good as send me my Tartan cloak. My watch is over for the forenoon. I mount guard again at 3 — at 9 and 2 in the morning. I have seen all the Palace by the Kindness of Mr. Marsh. You can send my cloak by Hector — or Peggy, if she wishes it, may bring it and she will see the outworks of the Palace. She can ask for the Celtic Guard and she will be shewn to where I am. I fear it is too cold else Joseph might accompany her.
Ever Yours
A. STUART.

From the Palace of
Holyrood,
½ past 2
Tuesday

A great number of Ladies are continually walking in the Park all round. If the evening is fine Maria & Mary Thomson might take a walk down and if I am not on guard at the time I would take a turn with them. The grounds are wonderfully improved. The Dukes of Argyle & Montrose we are told have joined us as common Celts & are to mount guard tomorrow.

Mrs Stuart,
28 London Street

— *A Stuart Story*, p. 20

Mary MacKnight, wife of
Alexander Stuart

In general, they are fully and even superbly dressed and arrayed in the belted plaid, each in his own clan tartan, which distinction gives a rich and barbaric effect to their appearance. Their grenadiers carry partizans and targets and are headed by Captain MacKenzie of Gruinard whose stately, and at the same time handsome and active figure, realizes the ideal of a complete Highland soldier. Here and there a white knee betrays the Southron or Lowlander – in most the limb is as dark as that of 'Glùn dhu' (Black Knee) himself.[3]

The society's important role in the visit served to publicise its existence and prestigious connections, but also to draw it into a very public row involving the flamboyant Alasdair Macdonell of Glengarry (1773–1828). Macdonell was a member – his name appears as no. 134 on the first membership list, paying his subscription in 1820 and 1821 – and had been treated with due respect. At the evening dinner after the second General Meeting in May 1820, his late arrival was acknowledged 'with loud cheers'; at the third such meeting, in September the same year, he had taken his place at the right hand of Walter Scott, who was in the chair, and one of many toasts that evening was to 'Glengarry, and the Society of True Highlanders'. Two years later this society (founded 1815) had formed a conspicuous part of the parade for the king's visit, with Glengarry at its head. Although it all seemed to have met with his approval, within days he had sent a long letter to the *Edinburgh Observer* which included a stinging attack on the event in general, and the Celtic Society in particular, suggesting that the majority of its members were 'masquerading' as Highlanders.

> I dined with them and I never saw so much tartan before in my life, with so little Highland material . . . Not being dazzled by outward show alone, I take this opportunity of withdrawing my name publicly from this mixed Society, for the reasons already assigned.

Glengarry's very public outburst forced MacKenzie to respond:

> The society was instituted on my suggestion in January 1820, and was neither intended to be, nor ever represented as a society of Highlanders . . . The Society is therefore open to every gentleman whose 'heart warms to the tartan' of whatever kindred, country, or religion.[4]

The row resulted in many column inches of comment in the press, offering an additional opening for those who were already objecting to the Highland focus of the event with its 'kiltification of Lowland Scots',[5] as well as for those who saw an opportunity to vent anti-Highland prejudice in general. Garth, himself a member of the 'True Highlanders', was not impressed. He told Scott that 'had it not been for Glengarry the king's visit would have passed without an angry word or unpleasant feeling', and referred to Glengarry's letter as 'a compound of vulgar style, malicious representation and uncalled for outrageous attack'.[6]

The society preferred to deal with the affair in private, and numerous meetings were held over a period of some months to discuss how best to respond. There was a strong feeling amongst some members that Glengarry's resignation should be refused so that he could be officially expelled, but in the end, as time had passed since the event, it was agreed, although not unanimously, to accept his resignation and draw a line under the whole business.

'I never saw so much tartan in my life, with so little Highland material': Alasdair Macdonell of Glengarry as painted by Raeburn 1810–12

One of the barbs Glengarry fired at the society was that it not only admitted Lowlanders but also 'foreigners' attired in Highland dress. This probably referred to Prince Adam Constantine Czartoryski, a Polish aristocrat, who had attended the General Meeting and dinner in 1821 as Scott's guest and was subsequently made an honorary member. At a meeting in 1823, Prince Czartoryski proposed Sir Samuel Osborne Gibbs for membership, seconded by Ranald MacDonald of Staffa. However, it was made quite clear by Staffa, possibly to deflect any comment to the contrary, that Czartoryski's participation in this way was quite legitimate.

He believed that the gentlemen were aware that this youthful Prince was connected with some of our noblest Highland families and he begged that he might now receive the authority of the meeting to assure his Excellency that the Society felt gratified by his having united himself to them and by his continuing to exercise those privileges as a member to which the principles on which the society was instituted, completely entitled him.

He was referring here to the fact that Czartoryski was directly connected to Catherine Gordon, daughter of the 2nd Marquis of Huntly. The Glengarry controversy subsided, and if nothing else, it had brought the society's existence and purpose prominently into the public eye.

In the wake of the king's visit, the Highland Society of Scotland proposed that an equestrian statue should be erected in Edinburgh as a permanent commemoration of the event, and subscriptions were invited to fund it. The Celtic Society asked each of its members to contribute a guinea towards a subscription. The accounts record that the final total collected was £52 10s, and list for posterity the names of those who had failed to pay up. In the end the money subscribed was not sufficient for an equestrian statue, so it was reduced to the pedestrian form that can be seen today

George IV's statue in central Edinburgh, for which the society raised £52 10s

20

Sir Walter's statue by Sir John Steell in Edinburgh's Scott Monument, for which the society raised 25 guineas

at the intersection of George St. and Hanover St. This was the first public donation given in the society's name.

Walter Scott had provided the organisation with its first taste of public pageantry, and he called on its services again in March 1829, asking 'as a personal favour' that some members would form a procession to accompany the celebrated cannon known as Mons Meg from Leith to Edinburgh Castle. In the evening a dinner was held, and replying to a toast in his honour, Scott expressed his warm sentiments towards the company: "Whether his life should be long or short, it would ever be to him a source of happiness to enjoy the friendship of such men as those by which he was now surrounded."[7]

His close association with the society during its first decade was remembered with great respect, and his contribution was formally acknowledged at the time of his death in 1832:

> From the formation of the Society Sir Walter Scott had always manifested the strongest zeal and anxiety in promoting the objects and interests of the institution, and by his unwearied exertions and constant attendance at its meetings both for business and conviviality contributed more than any other to its character and prosperity.

A subscription of 25 guineas (£26 5s) was later made by the society to the monument built in his memory, now a familiar Edinburgh landmark.

In 1823, having had two years in which to ponder how to further its objectives, the Celtic Society decided to concentrate its efforts on educational philanthropy in the Highlands and to incorporate the 'habitual wearing of Highland Dress' into the scheme. The General Meeting of March 1823 noted that the funds were already 'promising' but that 'until they become progressively more extensive' it would be necessary to limit any awards to 100 guineas. It was agreed to choose twenty-five schools in various districts across the Highlands, and to allow four guineas in prize money for each. In the first years of the competitions, three prizes were offered for excellence in Latin, Arithmetic and English, the best Latin scholar also receiving a silver medal. This limited range of subjects was soon extended to include Gaelic, Religious Knowledge, Writing and Geography. The regulations clearly stated that where two candidates were equally worthy of a prize, the one who was 'the better proficient in the Gaelic language' should be the recipient, and there is evidence that this rule was adhered to. The society thus exhibited its support for Gaelic from an early stage in its existence.

The key people at the interface between the society in Edinburgh and the Highland districts where competitions were held were the parish ministers. These liaised with schoolmasters and local members of the society. Also acting as examiners, they were obliged to submit written reports to the society, and these offer vivid insights into the competitions, which would often last for many hours. One such report from the Parish School of Ardchattan in Argyllshire, in 1824, the first year of the competitions, stated that the first prize and silver medal were awarded to Robert MacGregor, a ploughman's son, who excelled in the Latin examination. The same report indicated that the prize for reading and writing had been awarded to Flora MacCowan, and added that 'it is hoped that the society's regulations do not preclude *girls* from being candidates'.

The gender issue was also raised by John Norman MacLeod, one of the society's vice-presidents, in a report from the same year on the competition held in the Skye parish of Duirinish: "As some of the girls in the school were perfectly able to vie with the boys, we agreed that we should permit them to take their chance, and I trust the society will not be so ungallant as to censure our determination." While the terms used in referring to those eligible to compete were generally non-specific

– scholars, candidates, etc. – the clear expectation was that these would be boys. Initially, therefore, girls were included in the competitions somewhat by default, but to the credit of the society it did not take exception to this, and subsequently confirmed that 'any scholars either male or female' should be eligible.

In 1830, changes were made to the way the competitions were organised, when a sub-committee under MacDonald of Staffa reported on how best the society could use its funds, now in a healthier state, to encourage education across the whole extent of the Highlands. This report shaped the society's philanthropic involvement in education in the Highlands and Islands for the next twenty-five years. It was decided that the prizes offered would be in the form of books rather than money, and competed for across a wider range of subjects. Twelve districts would be chosen every year, each with a designated examination venue at which the best pupils from the various schools in the locality would gather to compete against each other. The new structure worked well, and it was frequently reported that the competitive inter-school element provided a strong incentive to pupils and teachers alike, inspiring both parties to greater effort. A report from Inveraray in 1834 quoted the testimony of one teacher that when preparing for the competition 'so keenly did some of [their pupils] feel the idea of being overcome by the children of another district that though they had several miles to travel home they would not leave the schoolroom till the approach of night'. The system allowed the competitions to reach more schools, and therefore attain much wider influence, as was highlighted in another report:

> The competition has given eight or nine teachers and several hundred scholars an impulse of which it is impossible to say how great may be the beneficial results; what then must be the benefits arising out of the aggregate of your exertions?

In the more remote areas where schools were widely dispersed, teachers and their pupils often had long distances to travel to the competition. A report from 1834 described the effort made by 'the aged schoolmaster' from Iona to reach Bunessan in the Ross of Mull, 'who [on a stormy day] with his young charges walked eight miles besides crossing a bad ferry although he might well be excused for trusting them to his assistant'. In places where distances and terrain were not so demanding, a sense of occasion was created by gathering the young competitors at a central point to march to the event:

> The several schools met at some distance from Kingussie, proceeded in a body with pipers at their head, through the village to the school-house. But in consequence of the great assemblage of people to witness the competition, the examination was held in the parish church where a great number of ladies and gentlemen were present.

A report from Fort Augustus in 1840 describes the schoolroom used for the competition, making particular reference to 'the superior school maps given by this patriotic society bearing its motto "Cha trèig mi thu", neatly suspended on each side of the room'. These had been produced by the society in the late 1830s, after a member drew attention to the fact that many small country schools lacked any maps to use for geography lessons. A committee had been formed to consider how the society might address this, and after some research it was suggested that maps could be lithographed for a comparatively small outlay and then varnished and pasted onto strong cotton. The first three decided on were of the Holy Land, Scotland and The World, and sixty copies of each were produced and distributed. These were followed by England and Europe. The project turned into an enterprise in its own right when the Society in Scotland for Propagating Christian Knowledge (SSPCK) offered to purchase a number of the maps for its own schools. Flushed with this success, the Celtic Society then approached other 'clergymen, school masters and private individuals' as potential customers. In this way the cost of producing the maps was substantially reduced.

Occasionally the reports from the competitions make oblique reference to the social and economic circumstances of the pupils, but writing from Islay in 1847, the Rev. Alexander Stewart was more explicit:

> In consequence of the prevailing distress in this, as well as in other parts of the Highlands and Islands, we did not think that the children who came before us exhibited their wonted vivacity and sprightliness but generally speaking they acquitted themselves very respectably.

Undernourished children are listless and dull, and the observation highlights the

Revd John Campbell
Kilchrenan Manse
Inverary

Edin^r 5 Royal Terrace
26th Feby 1850

Dear Sir

Mr Stillie, Bookseller, has by my orders, sent you a set of the Celtic Society's Prize Books, 35 in number, for distribution at the General Examination of the Schools in your District — I shall be glad to hear that you have received them in safety, and after your com= =petition I shall look for a full & satisfactory Report, with the view of being printed, should the Committee of Management so decide. I remain &c

Wrote in the same terms to
Revd Donald Jackson,
Kilmartin Manse — Lochgilphead,

Revd John Rose, Manse of Rosekeen Invergordon

shall look for a full & satisfactory Report': the secretary, Alexander Stuart, writes to Highland ministers about the society's school competitions, 26 February 1850 (the list of ministers continues down the page)

impact of the failure of the potato crop in the Highlands and Islands at that time. An earlier report (Badenoch, 1833) stated that although the people were poor, they 'made great exertions to give their children the advantage of a good education', and it is not surprising, therefore, that it was also noted that the prize volumes were greatly valued and often shared. The Edinburgh bookseller James Stillie sent a selection of books to each place where a competition was held; those in English covered a range of subjects including history, natural history, travel and exploration as well as religion. Those in Gaelic were less inspiring, and any pupil receiving the

Gaelic translation of Bunyan's *Pilgrim's Progress* got the best by far of a fairly heavy selection of religious texts.

The first two decades of the competitions were a particularly positive period for the society, and much of this was due to the success of its educational philanthropy and the interest it generated. While the competitions undoubtedly maintained and emphasised the class system, they created a context that inspired pupils and teachers to greater efforts and brought some modest benefits. Education was crucial to any chance of social and economic improvement, and the enthusiasm of parents and teachers was sustained by that understanding.

One exceptional result claimed was the example of Robert MacGregor from Ardchattan, who, as already noted, was one of the first pupils to be awarded the society's medal. As a result of the attention he received in winning it, he was encouraged to compete for a bursary from the Clan MacGregor Society, and this allowed him to attend Glasgow University to study medicine. He subsequently passed his examinations as a surgeon and took up a position in the Royal Infirmary of Glasgow. The minister reporting this success story concluded that 'were it not for your Society, it is not too much to say, that this young man would not have risen to beyond that sphere in which his [ploughman] father moves'.

MacGregor was a classic 'lad o' pairts' whose achievements depended precariously on a confluence of factors, including his name. His ability in Gaelic, specially noted in the society's competition, was later put to good use in contributing articles on social issues connected with hospitals and medicine to the Gaelic periodicals produced by the celebrated Rev. Dr Norman MacLeod.[8]

Before the 1872 Education (Scotland) Act, schools in the Highlands and Islands were run by a number of different organisations, mostly with religious affiliations, including the SSPCK, the Gaelic School Societies, the General Assembly, and (after the Disruption of 1843) the Free Church. There were also numerous other small schools charitably or privately run. Although the Celtic Society's competitions were facilitated by ministers of the established church, it was stressed that participation was not limited to any one denomination. This was particularly the case after the Disruption, when a large section of the established church broke away to form the Free Church. The event had considerable impact on the scheme, particularly in those areas where discord was most acute. Anxious to avoid any hint of bias, the society reiterated that its competitions were open 'to schools attached to every religious denomination' and that 'scholars from the Free Church Schools, should any such come forward, will of course be welcomed'. In 1847 the Rev. Donald Macnaughton was in correspondence with the society, and in highlighting the ill-feeling that existed between the two denominations in his own parish of Killin in Perthshire, requested that 'one half of the Prize books should go to the Parish Minister and the other half to the Minister of the Free Church'. This solution was not acceptable to the society, however, as it contradicted its policy of inclusivity, and when a similar situation arose in Contin, Ross-shire, in 1848, the secretary made that position quite clear:

> I observe that you do not take notice of any other schools than those of the Establishment. As the Competitions for the Society's Prizes are open to schools of all religious denominations, the Committee would like to know what other schools there are in the District. It is true *some* of these may not avail themselves of it but the Society's offer is free to all.

The Disruption had changed the momentum of the scheme, and as the years following it brought the failure of the potato crop in many areas of the Highlands, with severe social consequences, it is not surprising that interest in the competitions began to wane. In addition, the society itself hit a low ebb going into in the 1850s, with an associated drop in income. It was, however, the passing of the 1872 Education (Scotland) Act and the transfer of the management of schools to school boards that delivered the *coup de grace* to the competitions. They did not come to an abrupt stop, but slowly dwindled to a point where no applications were received.

ROYAL CONNECTIONS AND PATRONAGE

George IV's visit to Edinburgh was the first of several royal occasions to which the society added its colourful presence. When Queen Victoria made her initial visit to Scotland with her husband Prince Albert in September 1842, members turned out 'in the garb of the Highlanders' to salute her on her arrival as she made her way through Edinburgh to Dalkeith Palace. A day later, on her visit to Edinburgh Castle, they had a prominent position in the High Street when the Queen received the city keys from the Lord Provost. Newspaper reports described the representatives of the society 'in plaid and philibeg, and flowing tartan, each member displaying the badge of his clan, with their bright claymores',[9] under the supervision of the Marquis of Lorne as 'commander', with the Viscount of Dunblane, Campbell of Islay and the chief of Clanranald as 'commanders of divisions'.

Organising its personnel in military hierarchy and formation was a standard feature of the society's participation on such formal public occasions. In 1849, members were again in attendance when Queen Victoria and the royal family passed through Glasgow en route to Balmoral. Fully equipped to act as guard of honour, they had a prime position on the Broomielaw where the Queen disembarked, and were later at the railway station when she departed for Perth.

It was, however, in 1847 that the society was given its most exclusive duty. On this occasion, Queen Victoria and her family were spending a day at Inveraray Castle as guests of the Duke of Argyll during a cruise along the west coast, and the society was invited to provide an escort. The occasion attracted a flurry of new members, principally from the Argyllshire gentry, and seventy of them camped on the castle lawn for a week. The Queen later expressed through Argyll 'her pleasure and approbation of their loyalty and appearance', and describing the visit in her *Journal*, noted: "The Celtic Society, including Campbell Of Islay, his two sons . . . with a number of his men, and several other Campbells, were all drawn up near the carriage."[10] She was at Inveraray for only a matter of hours, so a week of preparation was somewhat excessive. As a result, when the accounts were presented at the AGM the following year, the fairly large sum laid out required the explanation: "Your funds have

8th Duke of Argyll: president 1845–50, 1859–60, 1862–84

28

ences in connection with the Queen's Visit, and the Society's

attendance on Her Majesty at Inverary—

As follows:

		£		
Expence of Conveyance to & from Inverary &c—		29	2	6
Account to Mr Young of the Northern Club for expence of the Society's Commissariot department _£ 119 7 6_ And price of Plate voted to him for his efficient services _21 . ._		140	7	6
Expence of fitting up Tents &c—		12	15	..
Sums paid to Pipers—		26	16	..
Advertising, Postages &c—		5	12	10
	Sum £	214	13	10

ence of fitting up Tents &c': the society's outgoings in connection with Queen Victoria's visit to Inveraray in 1847

suffered some diminution but your committee think you will be of the opinion that the occasion was one which fully warranted such an expenditure."

The society was always very diligent in formally expressing its loyal and patriotic sentiments towards the monarchy at significant moments – deaths, marriages, accessions to the throne and so forth. These events were acknowledged with an appropriately worded 'Loyal and Dutiful Address', written out by professional calligraphers, and presented to the monarch by one of the elite aristocrats in its membership, usually the Duke of Argyll. This was standard practice for many nineteenth-century organisations. The first sent by the society was to congratulate George IV on his accession in May 1820, and while the message followed protocol, it also incorporated what could be described as a 'mission statement' for the new organisation. It declared its purpose as 'for encouraging the use of the ancient Garb of the Highlanders of Scotland in the Highlands, and for preserving the characteristics of the Highlanders', and after the usual expressions of congratulations and good wishes, continued:

We feel these sentiments the more intimately connected with the purposes of our institution, because we are well entitled to boast that the ancient dress of the Highlands of Scotland has been long a badge of loyalty and fidelity to their King and Country and because in contributing to preserve the peculiar garb and manner of the primitive race we doubt not that we are fostering and strengthening their attachment to your Majesty's person and the constitution of Britain.

The text was Scott's, and his ideology of promoting the distinctive qualities of the Highland people within a British framework is evident in it, but this perspective was equally reflective of that of the Celtic Society in general. Similarly, the address sent to mark William IV's accession in 1830 referred to the repeal of the Disarming and Disclothing Acts, citing 'the paternal goodness of your Majesty's father [George III] obliterating painful recollections, and restoring to the Highlanders the use of their ancient garb and weapons'. It also recalled George IV's visit, highlighting 'his most flattering partiality for the dress as well as the people'. Seven years later, in acknowledging Victoria's accession, the society's main object was described as 'promoting education in the Highlands', indicating a change of emphasis. On the queen's marriage in 1840 it was decided to have the Loyal Addresses to her and her husband written in both Gaelic and English.

The society had access to the royal family through the aristocrats in its membership, particularly the House of Argyll. The 6th, 7th and 8th dukes were all presidents of the society in the nineteenth century, the sixth duke accepting that position three times between 1823 and 1839. After being made an honorary member at the 1840 AGM, Prince Albert agreed to become patron, the first royal to hold that position. In 1864 Prince Alfred, who had been present at the society's ball that year, followed his late father in the same role.

Queen Victoria's passion for all things Highland, not least for tartan and Highland dress, was given a broader perspective after her marriage to Prince Albert, who was interested in the

6th Duke of Argyll: president 1823–25, 1830–32, 1839

Celtic languages. This offered the society the opportunity to engage royal attention in its activities and purpose. The ultimate expression of royal approval was confirmed at a meeting on 28 July 1873 when the secretary read out a warrant received by Argyll, the current president. It stated that Queen Victoria 'has been graciously pleased to accede to the request, and to command that the Society shall be styled the "Royal Celtic Society"'.

7th Duke of Argyll, president 1841–43

22509

Whitehall
19! May 1873

My Lord Duke,

I have had the Honor to submit to The Queen the request of the " Celtic Society " of which Your Grace is President, that they may be permitted to assume the title of "Royal":–

And I have to inform Your Grace that Her Majesty has been graciously pleased to accede to the request, and to Command that the Society shall be styled the "Royal Celtic Society".

I have the Honor to be,
My Lord Duke,
Your Grace's
Obedient Servant
H A Bruce

His Grace
The Duke of Argyll
K.T.

How the Celtic Society became 'Royal': letter to the president, the 8th Duke of Argyll, from the Home Secretary, Henry Austin Bruce, 19 May 1873

Tartan, Celtic Balls and 'The Ancient Highland Dress'

At its first General Meeting in March 1820, the hope was expressed that 'the Celtic Society with the sister establishments for the improvement of Highlanders will walk in friendly congratulation amid hosts of Highlanders plaided and plumed in their tartan array', and newspaper reports on the dinner following the meeting noted the dazzling effect of the company gathered together in full Highland dress. Although the initial aim of promoting the use of 'the ancient Highland garb' throughout the Highlands was soon extended to embrace wider objectives, the emphasis on promoting the wearing of Highland dress retained a central place in the society's rhetoric throughout the nineteenth century.

The approach to addressing this concern had two aspects: encouragement and example. The regulations for the school competitions during the early years expressed the expectation that 'the holders of Prizes were to assume that [dress] as their ordinary garb'. In 1824, the first year of the competitions, it was reported from Dunvegan in Skye that the prize money had been delivered to the parents of the successful pupils 'under the express condition of its being applied to purchase Highland dresses for their children, which they will comply with, with pride and satisfaction'. It is not clear to what extent the matter was pursued, but as many of the children involved came from homes where there were many more pressing calls on meagre resources, it is unlikely that the condition could have been easily met. A report from the competition held in Killin in 1826 suggested candidly that 'this rule, rigorously acted up to, must materially diminish the beneficial results of the other parts of this excellent system', adding that it was 'considered an expensive dress', and pointing out that children from the poorest families, those least able to appear resplendent in tartan, were also those most in need of the society's support. In similar vein, a report from the school competitions in South Uist in 1834 stated quite bluntly that 'the circumstances and habits of the people preclude the possibility of conforming to the Society's regulations respecting the Highland Dress'. This clearly reflected changes in dress habits due to historical and social factors, and changes in the cost of clothing brought about by the Industrial Revolution.

In some cases, however, the regulation was more readily embraced. A report on the competition in Dornoch in 1835 expressed satisfaction in seeing 'the prompt manner in which so great a number had complied with the adoption of the ancient Highland Dress', stating that around fifty pupils appeared in tartan, while more than twenty boys were 'in the full costume of the Gael'. In one exceptional case, a report from a competition in Brodick, Arran, highlighted the fact that 'the greater number of Miss Brown's pupils with their spirited instructress at their head, attended the Examination neatly dressed in the Tartan of the 42nd Highlanders'. As time went on, the clause referring to wearing Highland dress at the competitions was retained more to honour the initial interest of the society than actually to implement it. Replying to a letter on the subject from the Rev. Archibald Clerk of Kilmallie in 1848, the secretary wrote that 'it has been for a good many years held to be a rule fully as much honoured in the breach as in the observance', and continued: "Like yourself the present Committee of Management, I believe, would like to see the Highlanders good scholars, whether they wear the kilt or the breeches." When the 'Rules and Regulations' for the school competitions were revised in 1832, an additional prize was introduced to be awarded 'to the *Adult* who shall constantly wear the Highland Garb of home-made tartan. The prize to be either a medal or a sporran of the value of ten shillings with a suitable inscription'. That year, one of the first medals in this category was awarded at the competition in Killin to 'Alpine MacAlpine, aged 75, who never in his life wore anything else'. Although there were others similarly honoured, it was only ever an occasional award, and before long it ceased completely.

As has already been described, parading in colourful tartan 'uniform' was a distinctive feature of the society's public duties. Another opportunity for the society to promote the wearing of the 'Highland garb' by example was at the 'Celtic Balls' it organised, starting in 1835 and held annually for some years, then more sporadically to the end of the century. At these events tartan was used in dress and décor to full effect. The balls took place in the grand surroundings of the Assembly Rooms in George Street, Edinburgh, and were described in one report as 'a leading feature in the gaieties of the Scottish Metropolis, attended by the *élite* of the nobility and gentry of the country'. The lavish display with which the venue was festooned for the first ball required 'between 600 and 700 yards [of tartan]' which, as was noted in the minutes to justify the expense, had been kept and would be used again. Reporting on the 1835 ball, the *Inverness Courier* observed that 'the stair-case and the lobby were fitted up with tartans of the different clans, the pillars were adorned with mountain heaths, in a simple rather than a splendid style, and quite appropriate and national'.[11]

The 'Celtic Fancy Balls'

Beginning in 1835, for many years the Celtic Society held annual charity events known 'Celtic Fancy Balls' in the Assembly Rooms, George St. – 'fancy' in the sense of Highland dress for the men and ball gowns for the women.

These events were underpinned by an elaborate system of etiquette. Those wishing attend, whether ladies or gentlemen, had first to present their credentials (via a servant, in person) to one of the 'patronesses' of the ball. This was presumably to ensure that on those of a certain social standing could attend. The patroness then signed and issued a lady or gentleman's voucher. These vouchers stipulated the appropriate dress code, e.g. 'The Lady Patronesses request Ladies to appear in Tartan – Full or Fancy Dress' (i.e. day-we or evening-wear) or 'The Lady Patronesses request Gentlemen will appear in Highland Costume – Uniform or Fancy Dress' (i.e. military or civilian).

Le Bal Celtiq

Only one of the women in d'Hardiviller's *Le Bal Celtique* (1836), the young lady on the right, is wearing any tartan. The specific mention of it in surviving ladies' vouchers (1837, 1841, 1844) suggests that fashionable females were a little bit reluctant to wear it, given that it was still associated with the kind of low-class Highland women seen on the streets.

Vouchers also explained how a ticket could be obtained, for example in 1837: "Vouchers must be exchanged at the Assembly Rooms, on Saturdays, 7th, 14th, and 21st of January, between the hours of One and Four. After which day, Tickets will be charged double Price. PRICE OF TICKET HALF-A-GUINEA." By 1844 this had gone up to a full guinea, late or not.

Nor was this all. Some surviving tickets are printed on the back: "Highland Costume uniform Full or Fancy Dresses only. Carriages to approach from the West only. Chairs from the East only." These last are sedan chairs, the trade in which was monopolised by Highlanders.

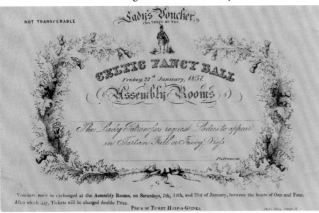

Voucher, 27 Jan. 1837, requesting ladies 'to appear in Tartan, Full or Fancy Dress'

Gentleman's ticket, 27 Jan. 1837, to admit Capt. Sinclair and a lady

The first ball produced a surplus of £300 to support the society's educational initiatives, and encouraged a repeat performance the next year, when the décor was themed as 'an ancient Highland baronial hall'. The scene presented was a mixture of antiquarian and romantic indulgence, with pistols, swords, axes and suits of armour grouped around the pillars, along with skins of wild animals, antlers and flags. Such was the interest in the transformation of the vestibule that it remained in place for a couple of days to be 'exhibited by gas light' to the general public.

The scene in the entrance hall at the 1836 ball was depicted in a painting by a French artist, Charles Achille d'Hardiviller (1795–c.1841), an historical portrait and genre painter of some repute who is thought to have studied under Jacques-Louis David. D'Hardiviller had come to Edinburgh with the exiled Charles X and his family when they were resident at Holyroodhouse in 1831–32,[12] and he taught classes from time to time in painting, drawing and perspective for 'the nobility and gentry' in a studio in George Street. In February 1836, it was reported at a meeting of the society that a request had been received from the artist for 'permission to dedicate to the Duke of Gordon and the Celtic Society a painting which he is in the course of executing and intends to have lithographed of the entrance hall of the Assembly Rooms fitted up for the Ball as a Highland Baronial Hall with groups of the Company'. The whereabouts of the original is unknown, but copies of the lithograph can still be found. It has the French title *Bal Celtique* and depicts two mixed groups in the decorated foyer, the men resplendent in full Highland dress. Unfortunately no information has been found to identify those shown in the picture, although it was suggested in a report in the *Oban Times* that Sir Donald Campbell of Dunstaffnage could be recognised by having the key of Dunstaffnage on his belt, and that the young lad depicted was possibly his son Angus. Captain William MacKenzie was present, as was MacDonald of Staffa, and either or both might be likely candidates to be included in such a grouping, but it is impossible to say with certainty. However, the painting provides a vivid image of the splendour of the occasion, drawing the eye past the imposing figures grouped in the 'baronial hall' to catch a glimpse of the packed ballroom beyond.

The balls were lavishly presented and overheads were high, but such was the élite clientele they attracted that there was still a surplus to be used for a benevolent project or donated to a specific cause. The 1847 ball raised £180 for 'the relief of the poor in the Highlands' and that of 1873, the last held for some time, contributed £105 towards 'the Endowment of a Celtic Chair in the University of Edinburgh'.

CELTIC FANCY BALL

Friday 1st March 1844

LIST OF DANCES.

1	Reel	Pipes	
2	Quadrille	Les Gondoliers	Musard
3	Waltz	Sophien	Labitzky
	Gallop	Les Huguenots	Straus
4	Quadrille	La Cloche Sonne	Musard
5	Reel		
6	Quadrille	Les Martyrs (2d set)	Musard
7	Waltz	Der Nacht wandler	Straus
	Gallop	Regatta	Lanner
8	Quadrille	La Fille du Regiment	Musard
9	Country Dance		
10	Quadrille	Napoleon (1st time)	Prince de Moskwa
11	Waltz	Die Debutanten (1st time)	Straus
	Gallop	Fortuna	do.
12	Quadrille	Le Rendezvous de chasse	Musard
13	Reel	Pipes	
14	Quadrille	L'Echarpe Rose	Musard
15	Waltz	Deutsche Lust (1st time)	Straus
	Gallop	Der Venetianer	Straus
16	Quadrille	Don Pasquale	Musard
17	Reel		
18	Quadrille	Le Quatre Heures (1st time)	Musard
19	Waltz	Jubel Klange	Labitzky
	Gallop	Hyacinthen Polka	do
20	Quadrille	Cent Suisse	Musard
21	Reel	Pipes	
22	Quadrille	Danois	Musard
23	Waltz	Die Fashionablen	Labitzky
	Gallop	Daguerotype	do
24	Quadrille	Krakoviac	Musard

Reels, quadrilles, waltzes and gallops: list of dances for the Celtic Society's ball, 1 March 1844

The emphasis given to tartan in the rhetoric attached to the Highland regiments in the nineteenth century, a perspective echoed by the society from its inception, was brought into sharp focus in 1881, when the War Office proposed that the individual regimental tartans should be abolished and replaced by a corporate pattern. The proposal met with a broad spectrum of opposition, and a petition against the change was widely circulated. The society was fully behind the protest, but had a certain sensitivity to consider, as the president at the time, who would have been the normal signatory on its behalf, was the Duke of Argyll, a serving member of the government. The treasurer, James Patten, took the decision to sign the petition himself on behalf of the society, and his action was later given the approval of the duke, who wrote that 'as a Member of the Government he felt himself unable to sign it but was glad that he [Patten] had done so'. In addition, a telegram was sent to a high-powered gathering on the subject being held in London:

> At a Meeting of the Committee of Management of the Royal Celtic Society held today it was unanimously resolved to express the Society's sympathy with the objects of the meeting to be held at Stafford House this evening and their strong remonstrance against the proposed change in the tartans of their Highland Regiments as going far to destroy the 'esprit de Corps' and pride of race which are the essential characteristics of the 'Highland Brigade'.

The society discussed the design of its medals in 1820, but it was not until 1823 that they were first awarded in the school competitions. This one (left) bears the legend CHA TREAG MI THU, a slight mis-spelling, while the button on the right (1835) is more correctly inscribed CHA TREIG MI THU

By the end of March 1881 the idea had been scrapped. There was, however, another protest in connection with the dress of the Highland regiments in 1884, which the society again endorsed, supporting the representation to the government against 'the proposed abolition of the feather bonnet in the Highland Regiments who wear it'. Both of these proposals to alter aspects of traditional regimental dress were reflective of the new ideas that were beginning to herald the modern era, a time of change that was, by the last decade of the nineteenth century, already starting to impact on the Royal Celtic Society in its dwindling membership and uncertain future.

'Cha Trèig Mi Thu': Support for Gaelic

The Gaelic motto of the Royal Celtic Society continues today as an acknowledgement of its long association with the language. Meaning 'I will not forsake you', it is from Joshua 1: 5 *cha dìbir mi thu, agus cha tréig mi thu*, 'I will not fail thee, nor forsake thee'. It may have been suggested by Stewart of Garth or William MacKenzie. Both spoke the language, as did quite a few others in the early membership.

The phrase appeared on the first medals produced by the society in May 1820, and a reference to MacKenzie's being asked to 'take the trouble of procuring a draft of the inscription intended for the medal' lends weight to the view that the motto was his suggestion. It was incorporated in the design for the special buttons produced for the society in 1835 at the instigation of the Duke of Gordon; it was impressed on the covers of the prize books awarded in the school competitions; printed on the tickets for the society balls; and generally used and understood as an expression of the society's purpose and benevolent intentions. A report, for example, from one of the school competitions in Fort Augustus noted that 'the competitors, out of respect and compliment to the society, had each inscribed the motto on the title page of their specimens of writing'.

As already noted, considerable emphasis was placed on ability in Gaelic in the school competitions run by the society. By 1825 it had been agreed that separate prizes should be 'expressly awarded to those who show particular eminence in Gaelic', suggested as a means of encouraging teachers as well as pupils, and thus 'to greater benefit the language'. An example from 1857 further illustrates this pro-Gaelic bias. It had been decided not to include 'pupil teachers' in the competitions

 **The Rev. Dr Norman Macleod** (1783–1862), an influential figure in the development of Gaelic literature in the nineteenth century, was chaplain to the society during the 1830s and 1840s. Well-known amongst the Highland diaspora, particularly in Glasgow, as *Caraid nan Gaidheal* ('the Friend of the Gaels') for his compassionate support towards those in need, he was also very involved with education in the Highlands through schemes administered by the established church. There is no record of his active participation in the society beyond being named as chaplain, however, a role in which he succeeded the Rev. Dr Robert Anderson.

on the reasonable grounds that 'they already stand marked as the first scholars, and have received the reward of their proficiency'. As an alternative, however, it was suggested that a special prize might be given to the best scholar among the pupil teachers, adding that 'with the view of a future supply for our Highland schools, the Committee would be disposed to make a knowledge of Gaelic a *Sine qua non*' – an indication that the society was not merely interested in encouraging proficiency in the language, but also recognised the need to employ Gaelic-speaking teachers in Highland schools.

One of the governing regulations for a school's eligibility to participate in the society's competitions was that it be attended by Gaelic-speaking pupils, and a selection of Gaelic books was included with the English books as prizes. In 1864, responding to a minister from Lumphanan in Aberdeenshire who returned the Gaelic books, asking for English replacements, the society agreed to the request but made its position clear:

> The Regulations point to schools in the Highland districts where it is not doubted that the Gaelic language, if not taught, is well understood; and had it been stated at the outset that none at your schools spoke Gaelic it might have stood somewhat in the way of the grant.

Books were occasionally donated to the society to supplement the prizes purchased for the school competitions, and in 1833 a generous donation of Gaelic books 'consisting of twenty-four copies of Ossian's poems and forty-eight copies of McIntosh's Proverbs' was received from Sir William MacLeod Bannatyne, a Gaelic-speaking judge. In addition, members of the society would occasionally recommend suitable books for prizes, as in 1835 when on the secretary's suggestion it was agreed to purchase 100 copies of the Rev. Dr Norman Macleod's *Leabhar nan Cnoc*, 'The Mountain Sketch Book'. When Macleod and Daniel Dewar published their *Dictionary of the Gaelic Language* in 1831, the treasurer, Joseph Gordon, brought it to the attention of the society.

> Although he had a limited knowledge of the Gaelic language he was convinced it was a most valuable work but it was doubly so to the Society whose aim always had been to encourage the study of that language amongst the natives . . . And as he thought it might be desirable for the Society at some future period to bestow premiums amongst the most deserving teachers as well as scholars, it would be an invaluable prize to them.

Approving this suggestion, it was agreed to purchase six copies, and these were then used as occasional awards for exceptional efforts by individual teachers whose pupils performed well in the society's competitions. In 1833, for example, a copy was presented to Archibald MacCallum, the teacher in Ardchattan, and in 1835 Miss Brown in Arran (already mentioned, p. 33) was similarly honoured, the copies having been specially bound and inscribed.

Providing grants to support Gaelic publications was to become a feature of the society's philanthropic activity in the twentieth century, but in the nineteenth most approaches of this nature were rejected as not being directly relevant to its purposes. There was, however, one successful application in 1876 from the publishers MacLachlan and Stewart, seeking a grant towards a new edition of Alexander Stewart's *Elements of Gaelic Grammar*, to enable it to be sold at a lower price. The committee agreed a grant of £50, reasoning that bringing the book within the financial reach of more people 'would be a legitimate application of the society's funds', stressing that the full benefit of the grant was to be used to reduce the price.

After the demise of the school competitions, the society was anxious to find an alternative project to encourage both educational achievement and Gaelic in the Highlands and Islands. With its financial situation looking much better in the 1880s due to improved returns on its investments, it was decided to start a bursary scheme 'to enable Gaelic-speaking youths who had passed the primary to complete their education at secondary schools'. The bursary was awarded for two years and was given on the basis of excellence in Gaelic, provided the successful pupil exhibited a

ELEMENTS

OF

GAELIC GRAMMAR

IN FOUR PARTS

I. Of Pronunciation and   III. Of Syntax
   Orthography   IV. Of Derivation and
II. Of the Parts of Speech   Composition

BY

ALEXANDER STEWART

MINISTER OF THE GOSPEL AT DINGWALL
HONORARY MEMBER OF THE HIGHLAND SOCIETY OF SCOTLAND

Royal Celtic Society Edition.

FOURTH EDITION REVISED.
WITH PREFACE BY THE REV. DR M'LAUCHLAN

EDINBURGH: MACLACHLAN & STEWART
LONDON: SIMPKIN, MARSHALL, & Co.
1886.

In 1876 the society awarded a grant of £50 for a new edition of the standard Gaelic grammar book of the time, provided it be used to lower the price

high level of proficiency in other subjects. Indeed, the committee formed to design the scheme recommended that 'a preliminary examination should be held in Gaelic and no candidate should be considered who has not previously passed in Gaelic'.

The society was able to attach its bursary scheme to the examinations for the bursaries awarded by the SSPCK, and in that way it was a relatively straightforward initiative to organise. Reporting on the first examinations for the bursary at the AGM of 1881, it was noted that upwards of seventy candidates had entered and sat a special paper in Gaelic, and of the two boys recommended, it was the one who had 'excelled in Gaelic' that received the award, although the other had been ahead in the rest of the subjects examined. The meeting heard that the successful student was now attending the High School of Glasgow, and as the scheme was therefore considered a success, it was agreed to continue it. When another candidate was chosen the following year, the society then had two bursars each receiving £22 a year awarded 'chiefly on account of proficiency in Gaelic'.

One of the unfortunate consequences of running the bursary in tandem with the SSPCK examinations was that under its rules, participation was limited to boys only. In consequence the society drew back from its previously inclusive gender perspective, defending the change of position:

> The original constitution of this society was not intended to include females within its sphere of operation but that exclusion was not afterwards strictly adhered to. It will not therefore be any breach of our original regulations to confine the proposed bursaries in the first instance to boys.

Despite this issue, the system worked well, and was a positive venture at a time when the society as a whole was at a low ebb, although its financial position was strong.

The Gaelic examination for the bursary was set and marked by Professor Donald Mackinnon, the society paying him four guineas annually for his work. After his appointment to the new Chair of Celtic at the University of Edinburgh in 1882, a prize was instigated by the society for the best student studying under his supervision. These interactions with the university were the beginnings of a change in the society's approach to its benevolent purposes that would, in the twentieth century, involve more interaction with the Highland community in Edinburgh, and with other Gaelic and Highland organisations concerned with promoting Highland culture and encouraging the Gaelic language.

George Malcolm Stuart (1868–1952) of Stuart & Stuart Solicitors, a grandson of Alexand
Stuart, served as treasurer of the Royal Celtic Society for many years. The follow[...]
reminiscence of him is by his son Malcolm Moncrieff Stuart ('Mike'):

"One enduring trait that may be recorded; he always dropped his voice when he got to [...]
interesting part of any conversation. It is said that he murmured something at a Heriot Tr[...]
meeting and only when the Committee read the minutes did they find they had doub[...]
his salary. That I cannot vouch for, but a friend of mine, on leaving the Club with my fat[...]
had something muttered to him to which he apparently seemed to agree. A day or two la[...]
he found that he had joined the Celtic Society which 'Stuart and Stuart' always seem to h[...]
run."

— A Stuart Story, p.[...]

Three generations of Stuarts *c.* 1908. Back row: Frank Osborne S. (1875–1965), Dr Emmeline Marie ('Lir[...]
S. (1866–1946), George Malcolm S., his wife Mary Elizabeth Scott Moncrieff (1870–1961), Herbert S. (188[...]
1943). Middle row: Marie Julia S. (1881–1942), Isobel Mary S. (1897–1987), Isabella ('Bae') S. (1822–1915, d[...]
of Alexander S. and Mary MacKnight), Malcolm Moncrieff ('Mike') S. (1903–91), Marie Louise Treloar[...]
1937), widow of Robert Laidlaw S. (1832–99, son of Alexander S. and Mary MacKnight), Charles Edwar[...]
(1865–1937). Front: Robert Laurence S. (1900–80). The three children are all George Malcolm's.

A Society in Decline? 1880–1900

For the last decade and a half of the nineteenth century the Royal Celtic Society was almost moribund. There is a gap of eighteen years from January 1884 to January 1902 in which no meetings are recorded. The account books shed some light on this period, showing that the society's investments were doing very well, and therefore it was not dependent on membership subscriptions to keep it afloat. However, very little else was happening: not an auspicious position in which to greet the new century.

There had been a previous slump in the early 1860s, when the secretary told the treasurer: "The Society is dying and will soon die a natural death. Something *must* be devised about the application of its funds to some special permanent useful object." Throughout the nineteenth century the membership moved around a lot, and there were often periods when it was difficult to ensure numbers were available to attend the General Meetings. Several of the aristocratic members were MPs, others were serving army officers, some were in the colonial service, and the result was that memberships frequently lapsed. By the 1880s annual subscriptions were in single figures, and by the 1890s they had dried up completely.

This decline was probably caused by a combination of factors: there was a distinct loss of focus and interest after the school competitions ceased; there were a number of other societies with broadly similar aims – the Gaelic Society of Inverness, founded in 1871, while having a scholarly purpose, also had its kilted dinners and assemblies and attracted a similar membership in its upper echelons, and An Comunn Gaidhealach, formed in 1891, was also supported by the Highland gentry; and there were numerous other examples. In addition, change was beginning to take place in the Highlands and Islands, and after a century that had seen waves of clearance, famine, emigration and migration, the land protests had resulted in the passing of the Crofters Holdings (Scotland) Act in 1886, signalling the dawning of grassroots social and political confidence.

If it was to continue, the society needed to find a different purpose in order to regain its former vigour and build a new membership in the modern era; it would be a slow recovery, but recover it did.

A Society for the Twentieth Century, 1902–1968

A New Beginning: Facing the Challenge

The first gathering of the Royal Celtic Society in the twentieth century was a General Meeting held in January 1902 at 56 Frederick Street, Edinburgh, the office of the law firm Stuart & Stuart. Those present were the Lord Justice Clerk, Thomas Cunningham (in the chair), Hugh Patten, J. Patten MacDougall, Joseph Gordon Stuart and George Malcolm Stuart. Noting that the bursary scheme was no longer functioning and that the membership was 'very small indeed', they debated whether the society had a future.

> After full discussion and consideration of the present position . . . and while fully recognising that the original objects thereof were now to a large extent met by the various Clan Societies throughout the country [the meeting was] decidedly of the opinion that it was undesirable to wind up a Society which had done such good work since it was founded in 1820, and for which they believed there was still room though in somewhat different lines.

At this significant moment the society needed someone with the vision and

Walter Blaikie was instrumental in reviving the society

influence to make it relevant in the new century while still retaining the essence of its aims. The man who would eventually meet this need, although it would be almost two decades before he fully engaged with the challenge, was Walter Biggar Blaikie (1847–1928), an engineer who had transferred his creative skills to publishing, and who had been in charge of the Edinburgh printers T. & A. Constable since the late 1870s. He was a polymath whose knowledge embraced science, history and the arts, underpinned by a liberal and public-spirited outlook.[13]

Blaikie was admitted as a member at the General

Meeting in January 1903, and took the chair at a similar one held the following year, then again in 1905. On this occasion, with only three people present, it was clear that little progress was being made, and the question of viability was again raised. The secretary proposed 'that the continuance of the society being impracticable and unnecessary it is desirable that it should be wound up and dissolved', and this might have been the end of things had Walter Blaikie not taken a stance in favour of continuing. It was therefore decided not to do anything 'towards ending the society in the meantime', and that the few remaining members should consider how the income could best be used to further its objects.

A meeting in February 1906 considered various responses, focusing on the 'best way of spending the income for the advantage of the Gaelic-speaking population'. A decision was made to reinstate the bursary scheme and to offer one bursary of £25 to support a candidate, male or female, for two years at any Scottish university. In addition, a prize of £10 would be awarded to the pupil attaining highest marks in Gaelic in the Higher Leaving Certificate, along with an honorarium of £2 to the teacher of the successful student.

These plans were directed at using the society's resources in a useful way, but no move was made to rebuild the membership. Another gap in the minutes between 1906 and 1920 confirms that the society had not moved forward significantly before the First World War halted any further development.

A Modern Society

The catalyst for regrouping after World War I was the centenary in 1920. There was no particular celebration, but the anniversary provided the impetus to call a meeting to consider once again 'if there was still work for the society to do' or 'whether the few remaining members should bring the society to an end and apply the accumulated funds to some appropriate purpose'. Blaikie was still involved, possibly now with more time on his hands. The main challenge was to build a new membership, and it was decided to reduce subscription costs in order to encourage this. A list was made of potential members, and invitations were sent to them with information on the society; in this way the membership began to increase.

At a meeting in 1921 Blaikie was elected president, and at last, in January 1922, the society was able to hold its first AGM since well before the war. It took place in

Dowell's Rooms, George Street, with Blaikie in the chair, ten other people present, and apologies from six more. The accounts from 1918–1922 had been audited and were accepted, showing a healthy balance of £2,508; new Rules and Regulations were approved, and the office-bearers and council were appointed. This was the moment the society embraced the modern era, reflected in a broadening of social representation in its management and membership. Blaikie was confirmed as president; the vice-presidents were Lord Seaforth, Neil Munro (the well-known author from Inveraray) and Sir John Lorne MacLeod (also a native of Inveraray, lawyer, Lord Provost of Edinburgh 1916–1919, and active in various Highland circles); the treasurer was another lawyer, G. Malcolm Stuart, who had held that position since 1908, and had a long family connection with the society; and the secretary was J. R. N. Macphail, sheriff of Stirling, Dumbarton and Clackmannan.

The members of council, a mix of middle-class professionals, including a number of Gaelic speakers and scholars of the language, along with two aristocrats, were John Bartholomew (lawyer, piper and antiquarian),[14] the Earl of Cassillis (a Gaelic-speaking lawyer who became Marquis of Ailsa in 1938), J. P. Grant of Rothiemurchus, Dugald McIsaac from Oban (a founding member of An Comunn Gaidhealach), the Inverness lawyer William Mackay (a founding member of the Gaelic Society of Inverness), Fred T. MacLeod (an Edinburgh lawyer with Skye connections, a writer of numerous articles on Skye, its history and antiquities, and a founding member in 1934 of the Gaelic Texts Society), David MacRitchie (an Edinburgh writer and antiquarian, founder of the Gypsy Lore Society and a founding member of the St Andrews Society of Edinburgh), the Rev. Dr Neil Ross (a Gaelic scholar and writer from Skye, active in An Comunn Gaidhealach), Sir Bruce Seton of Abercorn (author of *The Prisoners of the '45* and co-editor of *The Pipes of War*), J. K. Stewart (secretary of the Stewart Society), and Professor William J. Watson, who had succeeded Donald Mackinnon in the Chair of Celtic at Edinburgh University. This was a powerhouse of individuals, an influential body of 'movers and shakers' who had links to numerous other organisations and maintained the society's close connection with the legal profession.

Sheriff Macphail, like Blaikie, was a man of wide knowledge, erudition and experience, and theirs was a visionary partnership that was central to the recovery of the society. They had different skills to offer, but would also have had much in common, not least that they were both sons of influential Free Church ministers –

Dr J. C. Macphail had succeeded W. G. Blaikie as minister of Pilrig Church, Leith Walk, Edinburgh.

The strong representation of speakers and supporters of Gaelic on the council and in the membership of the society encouraged its continued support for the language. From 1922, the initiative to give prizes for performance in the Higher Leaving Certificate in Gaelic, started before the war, was revived and expanded, £5 going to those achieving the highest marks at all the schools where the exams were available. In addition, under the supervision of Dr Malcolm MacLennan, minister of St Columba's United Free Church, Edinburgh, books were sent annually to 'small schools' throughout the Highlands and Islands with the aim of encouraging the teaching of Gaelic, and prizes were offered for writing competitions in Gaelic in primary schools in the islands. Other funding at this time supported piping competitions and Highland dancing at the South Uist and Barra Highland Games, the Edinburgh Celtic Union Mòd, and the publication of the *Transactions of the Gaelic Society of Inverness*.

Sheriff Macphail took a leading part in the reconstruction of 1921

At Blaikie's suggestion and under his guidance, the society took on the responsibility of publishing Watson's iconic *Celtic Place-Names of Scotland*. Blaikie, a good friend of Watson's, stated from the start that he was willing to guarantee the project personally. The book, which has retained its prominence in place-name scholarship and remains in print to this day, was published in December 1926, and at the AGM in February 1927, the success of the venture was acknowledged:

> The Council desires to congratulate the Professor on the completion of his work, and to express their gratification at the part which the society has been able to take in the production of this very valuable and scholarly volume. Its reception, both by scholars and by the press, has been most gratifying, and the society may look forward with confidence to being able to assist in the publication of some other standard work in due time.

Members received a complimentary copy with a special cover and title page, and the society's involvement was noted by at least one reviewer.[15] A few years later a second publishing venture was undertaken: *Spanish John*, described as 'a narrative of the early life of Colonel John MacDonell of Scotus, written by himself', appeared in 1931, with introduction and notes by Sheriff Macphail. Again a special edition was made available to members.

Under Blaikie's influence the society developed its social activities in Edinburgh, holding invitation lectures in the 1920s. Papers were given by Blaikie himself on 'General Stewart of Garth and the Revival of the Highland Ideal' and 'King Arthur in

10th Duke of Argyll, president 1926–36

Scotland', by William Mackay on 'The Battle of Harlaw', by the Rev. Donald Lamont on 'Perthshire Men in Gaelic Literature', and by Sir Bruce Seton on 'Ladies of the '45'. The society was back on track, and at a dinner held in 1927, at which Blaikie spoke on 'Prince Charlie and the Highland Dress', it was publicly acknowledged that he and Macphail had given the society a new lease of life.

At the 1926 AGM Blaikie stated that 'he had now held office for 23 years and that he had no desire for re-election'. It is therefore clear that he had maintained his interest in the society through the doldrums between 1903 and 1920 and was then instrumental in reviving it in 1920–26. He died two years later, in 1928, and a poignant entry in the accounts for that year notes the cost of a wreath for his funeral.

Thanks to Blaikie, however, others were now involved who could direct the society onwards and upwards. In 1931 a revision of the rules took place under Macphail's guidance, and its main purpose was now broadly described as 'to maintain and promote interest in the history, traditions, language, and arts of the Highlands and Western islands of Scotland', with no mention of tartan or Highland dress. As part of this review, the position of 'chairman of council' was introduced to oversee the business of the society, and with this change the president became more of a figurehead. Macphail was the first to hold the new office of chairman, and the 10th Duke of Argyll agreed to become president, a position he then held until 1936. On Macphail's death in 1933 his important contribution to the recovery of the society was formally acknowledged: "He took a leading part in the reconstruction in 1921, was Honorary Secretary until 1928, and Chairman of Council until his death."

Without the leadership of Walter Blaikie and J. R. N. Macphail, the society might not have recovered at all.

A Modern Membership

Prior to 1922 membership had been in single figures, but a list for that year reveals twenty-six life members and sixteen annual ones; by 1923 there were forty life members and twenty-five annual ones. Membership continued to grow. Probably the most striking change from the previous century was the greater representation of the Highland clergy, many of whom were also Gaelic scholars and writers. They were now members in their own right where previously, with just a few exceptions, they had often been treated as mere associates. Those in this group included the Revs T. Ratcliffe Barnett, George Calder, Donald Lamont, Kenneth MacLeod, Norman MacLean, Neil Ross and Lauchlan MacLean Watt. Other notable members were the writers Neil Munro, Compton Mackenzie and Seton Gordon, along with the painter D. Y. Cameron. These lists of names suggest interconnecting networks in which Blaikie can often be identified as the common link. For example, he was close to the wider family of W. J. Watson and his wife Ella Carmichael, a circle which included the Revs Donald Lamont and Kenneth MacLeod. Watson provided advice on Gaelic place-names for Seton Gordon's classic *Highways and Byways* volumes, which were illustrated by D. Y. Cameron and published in 1935 and 1948. The members drawn from the aristocracy in this period were the dukes of Atholl, Argyll and Montrose, the Earl of Cassillis and Lord Macdonald.

If building a modern membership was what Blaikie and his new committee had in mind in 1922, then making some move towards involving women had to be given consideration. Few clubs and societies of the Victorian era allowed women as members in an equal capacity with men, and in the twentieth century most organisations were slow to adapt their rules. The Royal Celtic Society took its first step in this direction at the AGM of January 1922, when it was agreed to 'elect as Honorary Members ladies who have rendered valuable services to the people of the Highlands and Western Islands, or have materially assisted in the promotion of the primary object of the Society'. The number of 'ladies' was limited to a maximum of ten, and while they were not liable to pay a subscription, neither were they entitled to take part in administration. This was a standard format for the time: the Society of Antiquaries of Scotland, for example, used a very similar narrative for 'Lady Associates' adopted in 1901, and may indeed have provided the template for the Celtic Society.

No time was lost, and at a meeting in February 1922, three women were recommended for admittance as honorary members – Margaret Burnley Campbell of Ormidale (in south Argyll), Marjorie Kennedy-Fraser, and Elizabeth (Ella) Carmichael Watson. The three were good friends, and were well known in Gaelic and Celtic Revival circles; they were modern women who supported any new opportunities to increase female participation in public life. Margaret Burnley Campbell, who had learnt Gaelic, was an energetic force in An Comunn Gaidhealach, serving a term as president, and was a strong advocate for Gaelic within Highland schools; Ella Carmichael Watson was a Gaelic speaker and scholar, one of the first female intake at the University of Edinburgh, a founding member of the Edinburgh Celtic Union and Edinburgh Gaelic Choir, editor of the *Celtic Review*, and also active in An Comunn Gaidhealach; Marjorie Kennedy-Fraser was a professional concert singer, pianist and song-collector whose famous collection, *Songs of the Hebrides*, produced in collaboration with the Rev. Kenneth MacLeod, was published in 1909. They would not have been overly impressed at being limited in their participation as 'honorary' members, but equally they would have wanted to acknowledge a positive move in the right direction.

Although these three were the first female honorary members of the Royal Celtic Society under the revised regulations of 1922, the minutes reveal a twist in

Good friends: Margaret Burnley Campbell, Elizabeth Carmichael Watson, Marjorie Kennedy-Fraser

the tale. Almost a century earlier, at a meeting of the committee of management held in November 1836, it had been stated by Mr Andrew Fraser that when he and Capt. William MacKenzie were at the school examination at Clyne, the Duchess of Sutherland, who was present, requested that she 'might be proposed as a member of the Society'. The following week, at a meeting held to ballot for those who had been proposed as members, Campbell of Dunstaffnage, who was in the chair, began with the Duchess of Sutherland, proposing that 'from the very handsome manner in which she had requested to become a member, the ballot ought to be dispensed with', and the proposal was unanimously agreed. The rules of the society in the nineteenth century did not stipulate who could or could not be a member, only that 'candidates . . . must be recommended by two members and that admission shall be by ballot', and it is clear that, in line with the gender attitudes of the day, admitting women as members in any capacity was not ever considered. Therefore, if there was nothing to say that they could be members, neither was there anything to say that they could not. It is particularly interesting to note that the secretary, Joseph Gordon, was present at this meeting, and he for one would not have found the request at all palatable, given his dealings with the Sutherlands earlier in the century when they were ruthlessly clearing their tenants.[16] The matter, at any rate, passed with little public comment and the duchess died three years later. When the regulations were revised in 1924, the subject of membership was more specific, it being stated that candidates for admission 'must be gentlemen interested in the Highlands and Western Islands'. It was not until November 1973 that the doors were at last thrown open to 'ladies and gentlemen' on equal terms.

In 1923 the number of ladies in the society was increased to the full quota of ten when honorary membership was bestowed on Lady Elspeth Campbell (supporter of piping and Gaelic, daughter of Lord Archibald Campbell), Olive Campbell of Inverneill (aunt of Dr John Lorne Campbell), Sybil M. Macphail (Sheriff Macphail's sister, secretary of the Ladies' Highland Association, which supported education in the more remote parts of the Highlands), Lady Helen Graham (daughter of the

Elizabeth Gordon, the 'clearing duchess' of Sutherland: the first female member

53

The hilt of 'the most splendid broadsword I ever saw'. The sword was presented by the society to Sir Walter Scott in 1826, and displayed at the annual dinner of 1933

Duke of Montrose), Lady Helen Tod (involved with An Comunn Gaidhealach, daughter of the Duke of Atholl) and Frances Tolmie (the Gaelic song-collector and folklorist from Dunvegan in Skye). As can be seen, most of these women were active in support of Highland culture, and had current or past family connections with the society – in particular, Elspeth Campbell, sister of the 10th Duke of Argyll, who was adding to the Campbell aristocracy's long association with the society, and Frances Tolmie, whose father, John Tolmie of Uiginish, had been a member in 1821.

In developing a new membership, connections and links to past members were not forgotten, especially those who had been influential figures in the history of the society. At the unveiling of a large granite statue of David Stewart of Garth at Keltneyburn (Perthshire) in 1925, the Duke of Atholl stated that 'it was to the Stewart Society that they were indebted for the memorial, their efforts well-seconded by the Celtic Society', and both Blaikie and Sheriff Macphail also addressed the company.[17] In 1932, the society donated to the centenary events commemorating the death of Sir Walter Scott, and at its annual dinner in 1933, Maj.-Gen. Sir Walter Maxwell Scott of Abbotsford, one of the society's vice-presidents, was invited to preside. In acknowledging the important connection his great-great-grandfather had had with the organisation, he handed round for inspection the sword presented to the famous author by the society on 27 March 1826, referred to by Scott in his *Journal* as 'the most splendid broadsword I ever saw'.

The Royal Celtic Society flourished in the 1930s, lending its support to a range of projects and activities. The distribution of Gaelic books to smaller Highland schools continued, now under the supervision of Donald MacLean, headmaster of Boroughmuir High School, and the awards to those gaining highest marks in the Gaelic Leaving Certificate expanded as the numbers sitting the exam increased. Acknowledging the benefits of this initiative, a teacher wrote in 1938:

The Society's generous awards to candidates who do well in the Leaving Certificate Examinations is a very distinct incentive to good work. 'The Royal Celtic' has come to mean to pupils something very much worth attaining, and for its very effective support to Gaelic study I beg most sincerely to thank you.

Notable amongst those who received 'The Royal Celtic' were Angus Matheson, Derick Thomson and Sorley MacLean, who would distinguish themselves as Gaelic scholars, writers and (in two cases) poets. The society also donated £10 to assist the work of Carl Marstrander, professor of Celtic Languages at Oslo University, in recording Gaelic dialects, and this support was continued for a further two years.

A feature of the society in the 1930s was its close interaction and cooperation with other organisations that shared its interests, facilitated through several influential and public-spirited individuals who were frequently office-bearers across more than one organisation. Along with other groups with a Highland connection, the society contributed in 1932 to the fund towards the 'immediate action' needed to repair the memorial marking the grave of the Gaelic poet Duncan Bàn MacIntyre in Greyfriars Churchyard in Edinburgh. In the same year a donation was made to the fund to erect a memorial in Borreraig, Skye, to the renowned MacCrimmon piping family, unveiled in 1933. In 1934, when the Gaelic Texts Society was established in Edinburgh, the society offered its support by joining as a life member on payment of ten guineas, and the two organisations had several members in common – Fred T. MacLeod, for example, an active council member of the Royal Celtic Society, was also a founding member and first secretary of the Gaelic Texts Society.

As the 1930s drew to a close, the Royal Celtic Society could look back with satisfaction on a particularly successful and useful period in its history. However, the decade would not end on such an optimistic note.

CHANGE AND CONTINUITY: LOOKING FORWARD AND BACK (1948–68)

The successful inter-war years had restored the society to a position of strength from which it could look forward to a purposeful future, only to be frustrated again with the commencement of the Second World War in 1939. It would be nine years before it reconvened in November 1948 at a meeting held in the rooms of the Royal

Scottish Pipers' Society, York Place, chaired by Sir Francis James Grant, formerly Lord Lyon King of Arms. At this meeting, the loss was recorded of fifty-two members since the society last met, acknowledged by the playing of the piobaireachd 'Lament for Donald Dougal Mackay' by the honorary piper, Pipe Major William Ross.

The inter-war momentum was not easily recovered, and it took a few years to recalibrate the society's affairs. Meetings were sporadic between 1949 and 1955, the situation exacerbated due to the illness of both the treasurer and the secretary. The organisation still managed to function, however, and continuing subscriptions retained links with An Comunn Gaidhealach, the Celtic Union, the Inverness Gaelic Society, the Gaelic Texts Society, the Clarsach Society and the Piobaireachd Society. Support was given to the National Mòd when it was held in

William Ross, who played at the society's dinners, was one of the greatest pipers of his day

Edinburgh in 1951, and on that occasion the society joined others in organising a grand Highland Ball. Previous commitments to providing prizes for piping at the South Uist Games and North Uist Gathering, and for competitions at various local mòds, were also maintained. Specific projects to which the society contributed in the 1940s and early 1950s included the Culloden Memorials Restoration Fund, the publication of the *Kilberry Book of Ceòl Mór* by the Piobaireachd Society, and notably a sum of £250 in 1952 towards a new edition of the poems of Duncan Bàn Macintyre.[18] The society also worked with the Celtic Union to oversee and raise funds for further refurbishments of the poet's memorial in Greyfriars Churchyard. Despite this activity, the society's structures were not fully in place, a situation that was at last rectified in December 1955, at a meeting for all members held in the Goold Hall, St Andrew Square, when the following office-bearers were appointed to take things forward:

President:	Lord Macdonald
Vice-presidents:	Sir Thomas Innes of Learney (Lord Lyon King of Arms), Sir Compton Mackenzie, Maj.-Gen. Douglas N. Wimberley
Chairman:	Donald S. MacDonald
Treasurer:	Joseph G. S. Cameron
Secretary:	Ian C. Cameron
Council:	Sheriff Hector McKechnie, Hugh Watson, Hugo J. Patten, W. L. Stuart, Alexander MacFarlane, Rev. Angus Duncan, Gilbert McWhannell, R. MacDonald Robertson, John M. Bannerman

William Ross declined to continue as the society's piper due to his advancing years, but the young man who replaced him was a former pupil of his, John D. Burgess, who would himself become a pipe major two years later, and as well known in the piping world as his mentor. Although the society employed a piper during the nineteenth century and often hired additional pipers for its parades in that period, encouragement of piping through the donation of prizes only began in the 1920s and became a strong focus in the 1960s. 'The Royal Celtic Society Prize' of five guineas was awarded annually for 'the execution or teaching of piping or Highland dancing or the use of Highland Dress and the proper use of Gaelic Toasts etc in the Highland Brigade', and a prize of similar worth was awarded in alternate years at the Argyllshire Gathering and the Northern Meeting. In 1964 an annual prize was offered to the Laggan School of Piping, replacing the biennial prize previously given to the Northern Meeting, and in 1965 a suitably inscribed practice chanter was awarded to the best novice piper in the Queen's Own Highlanders, subsequently becoming an annual prize.

John D. Burgess, who played for the society, was as well known in the piping world as his mentor, William Ross

57

Support for Gaelic continued: donations were made regularly to various local mòds; a grant of £200 was given in 1961 to the University of Aberdeen towards a series of Gaelic textbooks, and in 1967 it was agreed that a donation of £25 should be made towards the publication of the poems of Donald Macdonald from North Uist, better known as Dòmhnall Ruadh Chorùna.[19]

Although the society changed considerably in the twentieth century from what it had been in the Victorian era, it was responding to time and circumstance rather than departing from its original aims. Its charitable activities moved from being predominantly focused on education in the Highlands to embracing support for a much broader spectrum of cultural initiatives with a Highland and Gaelic connection, often in cooperation with like-minded organisations. Membership in the twentieth century was more reflective of the Highland diaspora in the Scottish capital, and of a growing presence of influential Gaelic-speaking Highlanders in prominent positions. The focus on tartan and Highland dress became less important in the second half of the nineteenth century, and disappeared completely in the revisions made to the society's rules in the early decades of the twentieth. However, in 1949 another revision retrieved the clause 'to encourage the general and proper use of the Highland dress', thus picking up the founding principle once again.

In the spirit of its motto 'Cha trèig mi thu', the society's support for Gaelic was sustained from the earliest years of its educational philanthropy in the Highlands, and into the modern period. In 1935, when the National Mòd took place in Edinburgh, a dinner was hosted by the society on the opening evening for representatives of various Gaelic and Highland organisations. On that occasion the president of An Comunn Gaidhealach, John R. Bannerman, stated that 'the Royal Celtic Society had anticipated An Comunn Gaidhealach in almost everything and upheld the dignity and honour of Gaelic and the Gael when they were at their lowest ebb – they had done a great service to the Gaelic cause'.

Speeches given on such occasions are always generous, but the overall point was valid. At the time An Comunn Gaidhealach was formed in 1891, attitudes to Gaelic were taking on a more positive turn compared to earlier in the century, when derogatory opinions towards the language and those who spoke it were regularly aired in the press. Any promotion of Gaelic during that time encouraged more positive attitudes, and provided a degree of opposition to those who were keen to see the language disappear.

Towards the 21st Century: 1968 to 2020

Alan Hay

In 1968 J. G. S. Cameron, who had been treasurer since 1955, assumed the additional role of secretary, remaining in both roles until his premature death in 1990. Joe Cameron was one of the most influential figures in the society's history, and in his twenty-plus years in the two roles, he was the main driver of our activity. The society was particularly active at this time, and the council met on a monthly basis.

During the 60s and 70s there was a particular emphasis on book publishing. As had been agreed the previous year (see p. 58), £25 was given in 1968 towards the re-publication of Donald Macdonald's poems, and two years later a donation was agreed towards the publication of the Gaelic works of Katherine Douglas. In 1970 the auditor, Mr Huie, noted that the society's expenditure was very low in relation to its income. It has often been agreed that it is no part of our charitable purpose to amass large large sums, and a long discussion ensued on how best to make use of the money the society had accumulated. Council members Murdo MacLeod and Archie (AC) Macpherson raised the 'urgent need for certain books to be reprinted'. It is not, however, recorded which volumes they had in mind.

It is worth noting that there were two Archie Macphersons involved with the society during this period. A. I. S. Macpherson, whose nephew Angus is one of our most active council members today, was an Edinburgh surgeon, one of a talented band of brothers who included an ennobled government minister, a distinguished doctor, a decorated war hero turned businessman, and the captain of Scotland's first ever grand-slam-winning rugby team. AIS was chairman of the council for several years and subsequently vice-president. A. C. Macpherson was a Glasgow solicitor, teacher and ultimately university law lecturer. He was a notable character of great good humour, and a memorable raconteur. He was short, round and wore a most obvious toupee, all of which characteristics he regularly deployed in self-deprecating wit. He became chairman of the council in 1992 and remained in post until shortly before his death in 2015.

Beginning in the early 70s, the society began to adopt a less 'hands-on' approach,

Stuart & Stuart

In a remarkable case of continuity, the history of the Royal Celtic Society is inextricably intertwined with that of the Edinburgh law firm of Stuart & Stuart. As stated at p. 9, one of those present at the inaugural meeting in 1820 was a lawyer called Joseph Gordon. He was elected treasurer, an office he held until 1853 (see p. 11). He went into partnership with Alexander Stuart (p. 16), who served as the society's secretary from 1846 to 1864. Stuart named his eldest son Joseph Gordon Stuart (pp. 16–17) after him. In the next generation, George Malcolm Stuart ('Malcolm', pp. 44, 48) was a partner in the law firm, and also sat on the society's council.

Stuart & Stuart ultimately passed to Joseph Gordon Stuart Cameron ('Joe', 1927–90), a younger son of Joseph Gordon Stuart's granddaughter Josephine Gordon Stuart ('Bunty', 1883–1955), who had married James Douglas Cameron (1884–1973). Joe was the society's treasurer from 1955 and secretary from 1968. On his death in 1990 he was succeeded – both in the law firm and in the society – by his eldest son Joseph Gordon Cameron ('Gordon', b. 1957), the sixth generation of Stuart & Stuart partners to be involved with the society.

Gordon Cameron remains both secretary and treasurer today, linked by an unbroken thread to the first incumbent in his office 200 years ago.

Left, Joe Cameron with his wife Celia; right, their son Gordon

as we moved away from activity such as publishing books, awarding prizes and recognising achievement to become principally a grant-making body. These grants tended to be relatively small in the overall scheme of things, and the council took care to ensure the modest sums available were directed to where they would make a real difference.

From 1972 the society's support for publishing activity tended to take the form of a loan rather than a donation: publishing is, after all, a commercial activity, and the prevailing view was that funds were provided for the up-front cost of a project that should be ultimately profitable. A loan of £300 was advanced in that year towards the republishing of Alexander Carmichael's *Deirdre*, and a similar amount was arranged in 1974 to enable Club Leabhar (The Highland Book Club) to reprint *The Highlands* by Calum Maclean. In 1977 a loan of £300 (which seems to have been the standard amount) was made available to council member Iain MacLaren to publish a history of the MacLarens. These advances were charged at 5%.

The latter part of the 20th century saw several ambitious new initiatives in the fields of Highland language and culture. In 1977 a donation of £56 was made to the fledgling Sabhal Mòr Ostaig. The council minutes signal the intention that this should be a regular occurrence. A loan, at the usual rate of 5%, was advanced to the college in the same year, although it was converted to a donation (in other words, cancelled) in 1984.

The period also saw the growth of living history museums, institutions concerned with the preservation of a particular aspect of social or cultural history. The society supported a number of these, beginning in 1968 with a £10 donation for the Auchindrain Folk Museum, it being noted that it was 'in great need of funds'. Auchindrain would remain an annual beneficiary of the society for over twenty years, when the museum itself informed us that it was now self-financing. This is a recurring feature of the society's charitable activity, in that our funds have been used to assist with the early stages of a project's development, to help get it to the point where it can support itself.

Similarly, and also in 1968, five guineas were donated to the Glencoe and North Lorn Museum, as it was 'in urgent need of new premises'. Once again, Glencoe and North Lorn would be one of the society's annual beneficiaries for many years. In 1971 the Clan Macpherson Museum was added to the list, and it continues to receive a modest contribution every year. Contributions were made to the Clan Cameron House and Museum at Achnacarry until it became self-supporting.

Professor Ewen Cameron's lecture to the society on the Land Reform Scotland Act (1919) was delivered to a packed house on 9 September 2019 and shown on BBC Alba next day

Further one-off donations were made for individual projects. In 1977, £50 was offered for the repair of Duncan Bàn Macintyre's monument in Greyfriars Churchyard, although it appears that the planned work did not proceed (see p. 55). Two years later, £15 was voted towards the restoration of the memorial at Rogart to Sir John Macdonald, Canada's first prime minister. In 1984, £100 was given to the National Trust for Scotland for the repair of the war graves at Culloden. In 1986, special donations were made to Iona Cathedral and also to the National Mòd, on the basis that it was held in Edinburgh that year, just as had been done in 1951 (see p. 56). In 1999 a donation of £500 – a large amount by the society's standards – was put towards the purchase of General Stewart of Garth's broadsword for the Scottish United Services Museum. The society's prize-giving activity had not, however, altogether ceased, and in 1976 a silver chanter was acquired for the First Battalion, the Black Watch, for the winner of their annual piping competition.

The late 80s and 90s saw a growth in Gaelic-medium education, particularly at the Early Years level. At this time one of the society's main activities was to provide start-up costs for a network of Gaelic playgroups then being established across the Highlands and Islands. The society began to support Taobh na Pàirce primary school in Edinburgh, a relationship that continues today with the annual award of two Royal Celtic Society prizes at the school's end-of-year assembly, inaugurated in 2019.

The last fifty years have seen great social change and, not for the first time, the society has had to adapt to circumstances in order to survive. The admission of women on equal terms with men was first raised in 1972, when General Sir Philip Christison proposed that women be admitted as ordinary members. The debate rumbled on for more than a year, and it seems astonishing now that it was, at that fairly recent date, so controversial. At a subsequent council meeting, the minutes note that 'divergent views were expressed' on the question. The proposal was eventually accepted at a General Meeting on 13 November 1973, 'Mr A. C. Macpherson dissenting'. One assumes Archie must have moderated this view in

In 2017 the RCS helped organise the visit of these Flemish student journalists to Scotland. Their assignment was 'Scotland and the Clan System'. They are seen here with society member Mrs Elizabeth Roads, the then Lyon Clerk

'The Enchanted Harp': the society helped sponsor this children's production in March and April 2019

later years, as he never expressed that opinion as chairman; in fact, he was the chairman who welcomed the first female council member, Dr Mary Noble, a lecturer in anthropology at the University of Edinburgh, nearly twenty years later.

The membership remained largely aristocratic and professional in its composition, then as now containing significant numbers of clan chiefs, academics and lawyers. This has been reflected in the society's governing body. Following Lord Macdonald's death in 1970 he was briefly succeeded as president by Major-General Douglas Wimberley, before the election in 1973 of Sir Donald Cameron of Lochiel, who would remain in post until his death more than thirty years later. Lochiel was a very active president during his early years, often attending council meetings and 'presiding' in person. He was succeeded by Sir Iain Noble, that great champion of the Gaelic language, and in 1999 Sir Kenneth Alexander, a former vice-chancellor of Stirling University and chairman of the Highlands and Islands Development Board, became vice-president. In 1971, with the election of Brigadier Lorne Campbell of

Airds, we were joined by our only Victoria Cross holder. Another of our more noteworthy members was the Rt Hon. Charles Kennedy, the popular and respected member of parliament for Ross, Skye and Lochaber and leader of the Liberal Democrat Party, who joined in 1984.

Sir Malcolm Innes of Edingight, the long-serving Lord Lyon King of Arms, would succeed Sir Iain on his death in 2010, another link in the long connection with the Lyon Office which extends at least as far back as the days of Sir Francis Grant, Lord Lyon from 1926, who was vice-president. This connection continues today: Dr Joseph Morrow, the present Lyon, is vice-president and a very active and supportive member. Sir Malcolm was succeeded in 2015 by Sir Iain's widow Lucilla, Lady Noble, who remains our president today. HRH The Princess Royal, who has kindly contributed a foreword to this book, became the society's Patron in January 2020.

The society held an annual members' dinner during the late 60s and 70s. The minutes record a profitable buffet supper at the Signet Library in 1969, although these events soon moved to Surgeons' Hall, which became the society's preferred venue. These were the days before supermarkets and licensed victuallers offered the range of quality wines they do today. In 1971 AIS Macpherson proposed that the society should purchase its own wine stocks to supply its social events. These stocks were maintained for many years, carefully selected by Joe Cameron and his great friend, council member Dr Tony Lowther, both of whom were very knowledgeable on the subject and spent many a convivial evening with their chosen wine merchant, ensuring the quality was just right. (In 1821 the society had discussed a similar proposal, and a General Meeting that year was asked to consider 'the propriety of applying any part of the funds, at a certain rate of interest, in purchasing a stock of wine'. The meeting gave its approval, limited to sixteen dozen bottles of port and eight dozen of sherry.)

During the 1980s, however, social events became less frequent, firstly becoming biennial and eventually ceasing altogether, perhaps an indication of the ageing and, by definition, declining membership which troubled the society during the 1990s and early 2000s. Valiant efforts were made by several council members to arrange events around the turn of the new century. These included a successful gala dinner at Borthwick Castle, but they were otherwise met with limited success and, once again, the society had to reposition itself for a changing world in order to survive.

Alan Hay, the society's chairman, at the annual Culloden commemoration service, April 2019

Recent years, by contrast, have seen a number of well-supported initiatives. Membership has almost doubled since 2015. In 2016 the society embarked on a commitment to provide content to the Gaelic page of *The Scotsman*, on a three-week cycle shared with Sabhal Mòr Ostaig and BBC Alba. This activity ceased two years later with the newspaper's unfortunate decision to withdraw its Gaelic page, which reflected a tradition of publishing weekly or fortnightly articles in the language that stretched all the way back to *The Weekly Scotsman* in 1926. In 2018 the society sponsored a production of *Bàs Chonlaoich*, one of the great epic Gaelic ballads, at a conference in Skye organised jointly by the Celtic departments of the Scottish universities, reprised at the Scottish Storytelling Festival in Edinburgh. Another sponsorship was *The Enchanted Harp*, a children's production at the Edinburgh International Harp Festival, which marked the renewal of our historic relationship with the Clarsach Society. The society assisted with the heritage-based elements of the Royal Society of Edinburgh's *RSE@Inverness* programme, which ran across 2018 and 2019, and once again we are supporting the publication of historical and literary material related to our sphere of interest.

Regular events now include an annual Spring Lunch, speakers at which have included Dr Kristin Lindfield-Ott, Mrs Elizabeth Roads, Sir Thomas Devine and Dame Sue Black. A new lunchtime lecture programme was launched in February 2018, the inaugural lecturer being Professor Robert Dunbar, current holder of the Chair of Celtic at Edinburgh University, continuing a connection that began with Professor Donald Mackinnon, the first occupant of that chair, who was involved with the society in the late Victorian period. Appropriately, these lectures, now the centrepiece of the Society's calendar, take place in Edinburgh's New Register House, a building that stands almost exactly on the site of our first meeting 200 years ago.

Dr Priscilla Scott's lecture to the society on its own early history, held in the Dome Room, New Register House, on 16 March 2018, came as a revelation to its members

Some of the books supported and part-funded by the society since 1926, including *The Celtic Place-Names of Scotland*, *Spanish John*, *The Songs of Duncan Ban Macintyre*, *The Kilberry Book of Ceol Mor*, *The Highlands*, *Dòmhnall Ruadh Chorùna*, *Sàr-Orain le Catrìona Dhùghlas*, *A History of Clan Labhran*, *Sly Cooking* and *Tradition, Transmission, Transformation*

Notes

1   Hunter, *Set Adrift upon the World: The Sutherland Clearances* (Edinburgh, Birlinn, 2nd edn, 2016), p. xvi.

2   'Celtic society', *Glasgow Herald*, 13 March 1820.

3   'Notices of Chiefs and Clans', *Inverness Courier*, 29 Aug. 1822.

4   'To the Editor of the *Edinburgh Observer*', *Inverness Courier*, 19 Sept. 1822.

5   'From Blackwood's Edinburgh Magazine', *Inverness Courier*, 10 Oct. 1822.

6   NLS MS 3895, and see also http://www.jamesirvinerobertson.co.uk/DavidStewartofGarth Correspondence.pdf.

7   'Celtic Society', *Edinburgh Evening Courant*, 14 March 1829.

8   See Sheila M. Kidd, 'Gaelic Periodicals in the Lowlands: Negotiating Change', in Christopher MacLachlan and Ronald W. Renton (eds), *Gael and Lowlander in Scottish Literature* (ASLS, 2015), 143–58.

9   'The Royal Visit to Scotland', *Illustrated London News*, 3 Sept. 1842.

10 *Leaves from the Journal of Our Life in the Highlands* (1868), pp. 88–89.

11 'Grand Celtic Fancy Ball, Edinburgh', *Inverness Courier*, 11 Feb. 1835.

12 'Exhibition of Pictures by M. D'Hardivillier', *Caledonian Mercury*, 14 Apr. 1832.

13 *Walter Biggar Blaikie, 1847–1928* (Edinburgh, privately printed, 1929); 'The Late W. B. Blaikie: Publisher and Scholar', *The Scotsman*, 4 May 1928.

14 'Scots Sheriff's Death: Mr John Bartholomew, OBE', *The Scotsman*, 4 Sept. 1937.

15 Dr George MacDonald, 'Celtic Place-Names: A Scottish Survey', *The Scotsman*, 3 Jan. 1927.

16 See Hunter, *Set Adrift upon the World: The Sutherland Clearances* (Edinburgh, Birlinn, 2nd edn, 2016).

17 'A Perthshire Patriot: Memorial to General Stewart', *The Scotsman*, 30 June 1925.

18 Angus MacLeod (ed.), *The Songs of Duncan Ban Macintyre* (Scottish Gaelic Texts Society, 1952).

19 *Dòmhnall Ruadh Chorùna* (Glasgow: Gairm, 1969).

Addendum

When this book was in proof in December 2019, the secretary of the Royal Celtic Society, Gordon Cameron of Stuart & Stuart Solicitors, rediscovered the stamp long used by his predecessors for sealing letters in wax. It bears the figure of a Highlander and the Gaelic motto, as on the medal and button shown at p. 38. According to the minutes, its last outing was in 1968, when Gordon's father Joseph G. S. Cameron handed it round for council members to look at.

The RCS coat of arms, granted by the Lord Lyon in 2017, retains the motto but not the figure, which was felt to be old-fashioned. The arms are based on Celtic stonework drawn from a slapstone at Kilmartin in Argyll, surmounted by the saltire to symbolise the pan-Scottish nature of the society's modern-day activities.

Thanks

I would like to acknowledge the assistance of a number of people who have helped in the making of this book. My sincere thanks to Ronald Black who has drafted the content of the 'boxes' and carefully directed the entire project from start to finish. I have appreciated his expert guidance and good humour. Alan Hay has also been in the editorial loop and I am grateful for his helpful comments and encouragement, and for contributing the chapter on the society in recent years. Thanks also to: Máire Black, Dr Ulrike Hogg and the staff of Special Collections in the National Library of Scotland, and Professor Hugh Cheape. Finally, I wish the Royal Celtic Society well for its bicentenary year: Mealaibh ur naidheachd – buaidh agus piseach leibh.

Priscilla Scott

Picture Credits

4 Reproduced with the permission of the National Library of Scotland. **10** *The Edinburgh of John Kay*, p. 138. **11** Goodwood House (by George Sanders). **12** NLS Acc. 13898, no. 1, p. 11. **13** Trustees of the The Black Watch Regimental Museum, Perth (by James M. Scrymgeour). **14** NLS Acc. 13898, no. 1, p. 1. **15** National Galleries of Scotland. **16** Nicoll et al., *A Stuart Story*, p. 10. **17** *ibid.*, p. 11. **19** National Galleries of Scotland. **20** Internet. **21** *ibid.* **25** NLS Acc. 13898, no. 13, p. 68. **28** Inveraray Castle © Duke of Argyll. **29** NLS Acc. 13898, no. 6. **30** Inveraray Castle © Duke of Argyll. **31 (a)** *ibid.* **(b)** Thanks to Gordon Cameron. **34** City of Edinburgh Council Libraries: Capital Collections. **35 (a)** *ibid.* **(b)** *ibid.* **37** *ibid.* **38 (a)** Katherine de Jonckheere. **(b)** Nicolas Magnon. **40** Archibald Clerk, *Caraid nan Gaidheal*, frontispiece. **42** Alexander Stewart, *Elements of Gaelic Grammar*, title-page. **44** Nicoll et al., *A Stuart Story*, p. 70. **46** *Walter Biggar Blaikie* (Edinburgh, 1929), frontispiece, photo by James Balmain, Edinburgh, 1925. **49** *Highland Papers* vol. 4 (Scottish History Society, 1934), frontispiece. **50** Inveraray Castle © Duke of Argyll. **52 (a)** *Souvenir and Handbook of Feill a' Chomuinn Ghaidhealaich* (1907), p. 17. **(b)** University of Edinburgh (by Charles Hodge Mackie). **(c)** National Galleries of Scotland (by John Duncan). **53** National Galleries of Scotland (by Samuel Freeman). **54** Abbotsford House (photo by Kirsty Archer-Thomson, thanks also to Stuart Allan). **56** Thanks to Stuart Letford and Barnaby Brown. **57** do. **60 (a)** Thanks to Gordon Cameron. **(b)** do. **62** BBC Alba. **63** Thanks to Alan Hay. **64** Photo by William John Davidson with permission of Edinburgh International Harp Festival. **66** Gordon Casely. **67** Alan Hay. **68** Thanks to Greg MacThòmais (deputy librarian, Sabhal Mòr Ostaig), Dr Domhnall Uilleam Stiùbhart, Priscilla Scott and Máire Black.

Bibliography

Black, Ronald, 'The Gaelic Academy: The Cultural Commitment of The Highland Society of Scotland', in *Scottish Gaelic Studies*, 14/2 (1986), 1–38

'British Newspaper Archive', https://www.britishnewspaperarchive.co.uk

Cheape, Hugh, *Tartan: The Highland Habit* (Edinburgh: NMS, 2006)

'History of Bute House: Home to the First Minister of Scotland', https://historyatrandom.wordpress. com/2012/11/23/the-history-of-bute-house-home-to-the-first-minister-of-scotland

Hunter, James, *Set Adrift Upon the World: The Sutherland Clearances* (Edinburgh: Birlinn, 2016)

'Journal of Sir Walter Scott', http://www.gutenberg.org/ebooks/14860

Kay, John, *A Series of Original Portraits and Caricature Etchings*, 2 vols (Edinburgh: Adam & Charles Black, 1877)

Kidd, Sheila M., 'Gaelic Periodicals in the Lowlands: Negotiating Change' in *Gael and Lowlander in Scottish Literature: Cross-currents in Scottish Writing in the Nineteenth Century*, ed. by Christopher MacLachlan and Ronald W. Renton (Glasgow, 2015)

Mac Intoisich, Donncha, *Co-Chruinneach dh' Orain Thaghte Ghaeleach* (Edinburgh: John Elder, 1831)

Melvin, Eric, *The Edinburgh of John Kay* (Edinburgh: Eric Melvin, 2017)

Newton, Michael, *Warriors of the Word: The World of the Scottish Highlanders* (Edinburgh: Birlinn, 2009)

Nicoll, Isobel M., Stuart, M. M., and Cameron, Joseph G. S., *A Stuart Story as Told by Some Descendants for Their Descendants* (Cupar: privately printed, 1981)

Osborne, Brian D., *The Last of the Chiefs: Alasdair Ranaldson Macdonell of Glengarry* (Glendaruel: Argyll Publishing, 2001)

Pittock, Murray (ed.), *The Edinburgh Companion to Scottish Romanticism* (Edinburgh: ASLS, 2011)

Prebble, John, *The King's Jaunt: George IV in Scotland, August 1822* (London: Collins, 1988)

Robertson, James Irvine, *The First Highlander: Major-General David Stewart of Garth* (East Linton: Tuckwell Press, 1998)

Robertson, James Irvine, 'Correspondence of David Stewart of Garth', http://www.jamesirvinerobertson.co.uk/DavidStewartofGarthCorrespondence.pdf

Royal Celtic Society Papers, NLS Acc. 13898

Smailes, Helen E., 'Charles Achille d'Hardiviller: From Bourbon Image Consultant to Edinburgh Drawing-Master', in *Journal of the Scottish Society for Art History*, 18 (2013–14), 28–39

Walter Biggar Blaikie, 1847–1928: A collection of memorial notices. With portraits (Edinburgh: privately printed, 1929)

Priscilla Scott lives in the Scottish Borders but grew up in Argyll with Gaelic roots in Harris and Skye. She graduated in Celtic Studies from the University of Edinburgh as a mature student in 2007, continuing on to complete her PhD in 2013. Her main research interest is in the social history and literature of the Gaelic-speaking people, and women in particular, in the nineteenth and early twentieth century.